Fed by
God's Grace

D1522202

Fed by
God's Grace

COMMUNION
PRAYERS for
Year A

Michael E. Dixon
Sandy Dixon

Chalice Press®
St. Louis, Missouri

All scripture quotations, unless otherwise indicated, are from the *New Revised Standard Version Bible,* copyright 1989, division of Christian Education of the National Council of the Churches of Christ in the United States of America. Used by permission.

Cover design: Elizabeth Wright
Cover art: Detail from window by Francis Deck at St. Agnes
        Church, Springfield, Ill. Photo © the Crosiers.
Interior design: Elizabeth Wright

This book is printed on acid-free, recycled paper.

Visit Chalice Press on the World Wide Web at
www.chalicepress.com

10 9 8 7 6 5 4 3 2 1   01 02 03 04 05 06

Library of Congress Cataloging–in–Publication Data

Dixon, Michael E.
    Fed by God's grace : communion prayers for year A / Michael E.
Dixon and Sandy Dixon.
        p.   cm.
    Includes index.
    ISBN 0-8272-1029-9 (pbk. : alk. paper)
    1. Eucharistic prayers.   2. Common lectionary (1992) I. Title.
BV825.54 .D57 2001
264'.13–dc21   2001000762

Printed in the United States of America

Contents

Introduction

January 1, 2001. We realized this evening as we wrote the last two prayers for this collection of three volumes of communion prayers, that these were the last ones. Three years of work have gone into these prayers. There is a sense of completion, of pride, and yet the grief of an ending.

Sitting down at the computer, each time we read the texts for a given Sunday, we asked for God's guidance as we put our fingers to the keyboard to form words…that God would inspire us as we took these scriptures, interpreted them, and put them into thoughts for the table. And we felt God's presence as we wrote.

For those of you who have used the other volumes and have commented upon their helpfulness, we are grateful! And we pray that this final volume will help guide your thoughts at the table.

Fed by God's Grace, Year A is one of three books published for those of you who are called on to pray aloud at Christ's table. We hope that these prayers will serve as promptings, models, or clues to give you input as you prepare your own prayers. If they stimulate your thoughts, sharpen your insights, and focus your attention, they will serve their purposes. If, on some Sundays, you want to use the prayers as written here, adopting these words as your own, that's all right, too.

Many previous books of communion prayers have followed a single model, such as separate prayers for the bread and the cup. *Fed by God's Grace* offers four prayers for each Sunday: one for the bread, one for the cup, a unified prayer for both bread and cup, and a closing prayer to be used after the communion service.

That way, you can choose the model that is best for your congregation.

We offer these suggestions on how to prepare for praying at the Lord's table.

- If your congregation uses the Revised Common Lectionary, check to see what Sunday of the church year you will be praying, then find the appropriate page in this book.
- If your congregation does not use the Revised Common Lectionary, it may follow the general seasons of the church year. Find a set of prayers appropriate to the season.
- If your congregation does not use the Revised Common Lectionary and you want to choose a prayer that connects with the scripture lesson for the day, use the scripture index in the back of the book.
- When you have selected a prayer, read and reflect on all the scripture readings at the top of the page. This is a part of your spiritual preparation for serving at the table and can help you understand the concepts behind the prayer.
- Read the prayer to yourself (and to God), as spiritual preparation and rehearsal. Revise the prayer as necessary to fit your own beliefs or those of your congregation or denomination, and to fit any particular contexts of your local situation. Write out the prayer, make notes, or commit it to memory, as is right for you.
- Before the service begins, take a few moments of silent prayer and reflection or take time to pray together with others who are leading worship.

- If you are one who plans the worship service, you have permission to quote individual prayers in your congregation's worship bulletins. People who have used the books have mentioned that it was helpful to print the Prayers after Communion in the bulletin as unison prayers.
- Sometimes the prayers quote a verse or more of a hymn. These can be read by the person leading prayer, or they can be sung by the congregation or choir.

As mentioned above, these collections of prayers for the communion table follow the seasons of the church year. The church year begins with Advent, the season of preparation before Christmas. From there we move into Epiphany, Lent, Eastertide, and finally Pentecost, the longest season of the church year. The Revised Common Lectionary, a three-year cycle of scripture readings increasingly being used in many congregations, follows a progression of scripture passages designed to give the minister and congregation an overview of the Bible: Hebrew Scriptures, psalms, epistles and gospels. For Year A, the major gospel is Matthew, year B Mark and year C Luke. All three years use John.

Prayers in *Fed by God's Grace* pick their eucharistic themes from the scriptures. Not every scripture is used in each Sunday's sets of prayers, but we tried to touch base with the themes, if not the words, of each set of scripture texts.

We have used as our source of scripture listings *The Revised Common Lectionary,* developed by the Consultation on Common Texts, published in 1992. Following the lectionary plan, this book has built in all the variables for the calendar years. Confusingly, not all the seasons are the same length from year to year. Lent counts forty days backward from the date of Easter, and Pentecost falls seven Sundays after Easter. Since Easter moves, Epiphany may be very short and Pentecost very long in a given year, or Epiphany will be longer and Pentecost shorter in another year. You might want to check with the pastor to see what Sunday of the church year you will be serving at the table.

Since the church year begins with the first Sunday in Advent in late November or early December, we offer the following chart so that you will know when to use these books.

Year A

Advent 2001—last Sunday of Pentecost 2002
Advent 2004—last Sunday of Pentecost 2005
Advent 2007—last Sunday of Pentecost 2008
Advent 2010—last Sunday of Pentecost 2011

Year B

Advent 2002—last Sunday of Pentecost 2003
Advent 2005—last Sunday of Pentecost 2006
Advent 2008—last Sunday of Pentecost 2009
Advent 2011—last Sunday of Pentecost 2012

Year C

Advent 2003—last Sunday of Pentecost 2004
Advent 2006—last Sunday of Pentecost 2007
Advent 2009—last Sunday of Pentecost 2010
Advent 2012—last Sunday of Pentecost 2013

On a personal note, it is always so amazing to see ways that God's grace abounds! The years we have been writing these books of prayers have been filled with some special sorrows. Each of us has lost a parent in these three years. These have been occasions filled with grief and despair.

Yet in the midst of the grief and despair, we feel God's grace at work. We feel the prayers of our families, our friends, and colleagues.

And we are once more blessed by grace.

Writing these books has been an exercise filled with grace. The last prayer Sandy wrote was for the sixth Sunday of Easter. Psalm 66 was one of the texts: "But truly God has listened; he has given heed to the words of my prayer. Blessed be God, because he has not rejected my prayer or removed his steadfast love from me" (vv. 19–20).

May all our readers truly feel that they are fed by God's grace.

Mike and Sandy
January 2001

First Sunday of Advent

Isaiah 2:1–5
Psalm 122
Romans 13:11–14
Matthew 24:36–44

PRAYER FOR THE BREAD: On this first Sunday of Advent, we think we know what time it is. All the ads and commercials tell us it is time to get ready for Christmas. It is time to want, shop, purchase, clean, and cook for the holidays.

Yet we are taken aback when we really listen to your Word for today. For the *time* is about salvation, light, and living honorably. These emphases remind us of how we are to get ready to celebrate your coming as the child Jesus, and your coming again.

Jesus, we thank you for your life and death, which made possible the resurrection and life eternal. Wake us now into life anew as we wait for you. Let this bread, your body, give us strength to ready the world for you. Amen.

PRAYER FOR THE CUP: God of light, in a world filled with uncertainty, we come to this sacred table today. We have heard your words telling us to prepare, for we do not know when you are coming. We have heard your words telling us how to live lives worthy of our Savior. In this uncertain world, you have given us guidelines.

We see the light of the first Advent candle; it gives us hope in a dark world. We see the cup on this table; it gives us life in a finite world. We are given the gift of life

eternal in this cup by the life, death, and resurrection of
the Son of Man.

As we drink from this cup, we receive the strength
to walk in the light. Amen.

UNIFIED PRAYER:
> O God of goodness, peace, and light,
> we come to your table today seeking
> the peace you want for your people.
> Help us make our swords into plowshares
> that we may nurture the earth and plant.
> Show us how to turn our spears into pruning hooks,
> that we may reap bountifully.
> With the abundance of your feast set before us,
> the bread harvested from the wheat,
> the grapes from the vines,
> we remember your gift to us
> in your Son, Jesus Christ.
> In this season of preparation, let us
> walk in goodness and light. Amen.*

PRAYER AFTER COMMUNION: Because we are here in your
house of worship, O God of all good things, we know
that you have already come. Again, though, we celebrate
Advent in thanksgiving—and anticipate your coming
again in Christ to complete what you have already begun.
We go forth looking to the light! Amen.

*Sandy Dixon, *Everlasting Light* (St. Louis: Chalice Press, 2000), p. 14.

Second Sunday of Advent

Isaiah 11:1–10
Psalm 72:1–7, 18–19
Romans 15:4–13
Matthew 3:1–12

PRAYER FOR THE BREAD: God of steadfastness and encouragement, guide us to live in the harmony of Jesus Christ. In this Advent season, we hear many conflicting claims for our attention and loyalty. Help these silent moments of communion be a time when we can hear your voice, a time when we can give you glory and praise. The bread we offer reminds us of the Christ, who offered his body for our sakes. Help us open our hearts to the joy and peace that your Spirit gives. Amen.

PRAYER FOR THE CUP: We are at this holy table serving you, Wondrous God, who can create a place where wolves and lambs live together, and where a child shall lead a parade of wild beasts. You can create a new heaven and a new Earth. Then you can forgive all our sin and restore our brokenness. The cup that we are about to take is all about restoring brokenness, for it is your Son's brokenness that makes us whole. We drink from the cup, and in Jesus, the Christ, you act in love to make all things new. Thanks be to God!*

---

*Adapted from Linda McKiernan-Allen, ed., *Celebrating Incarnation* (St. Louis: Chalice Press, 2000), p. 54.

Unified Prayer:

Lo, how a rose e'er blooming from tender stem
hath sprung,
of Jesse's lineage coming by faithful prophets sung;
it came a flow'ret bright, amid the cold of winter
when half spent was the night.
Isaiah 'twas foretold it, the rose I have in mind;
with Mary we behold it, the virgin mother kind.
To show God's love aright she bore to us a
Savior when halfspent was the night.[*]

Blessed are you, God, for the wondrous things you have done for your people. You have sent to us a Savior in your Son, Jesus Christ. We celebrate the greatness of your love in coming to this table today. The bread and cup, the body and blood of your Son are given to us by your grace. In the presence of the Holy Spirit, let us eat and drink these emblems set before us. Amen.[**]

Statement after Communion:

"Children of God, arise!
Go from this place nourished by bread and cup,
inspired by a vision of God's peace,
eager to live 'as if' the whole world were God's
holy mountain,
where no one will ever again hurt or destroy."[***]

---

[*]"Lo, How a Rose E'er Blooming," German carol (15th century), trans. Theodore Baker (1894).
[**]Dixon, *Everlasting Light,* p. 18.
[***]McKiernan-Allen, ed., *Celebrating Incarnation,* p. 61.

Third Sunday of Advent

Isaiah 35:1–10
Psalm 146:5–10 or *Luke 1:47–55*
James 5:7–10
Matthew 11:2–11

PRAYER FOR THE BREAD: O God who plants seeds in the desert to see them bloom, enter our spiritual desert. Plant within us the seeds of promise and hope. Help us to blossom into Christians who show our faith by our actions.

You have acted in our behalf by sending us your Son, Jesus, to be our Savior. We have accepted this gift of grace. The bread on this table is an earthly symbol of that gift—the body of our Savior. As we eat of this bread, help our spiritual desert come to life that we may share the good news with all your children. Amen.

PRAYER FOR THE CUP: The scriptures nearly shout this day the message of good news! Things that are wrong will be righted. Miracles will happen. In your reign, mighty and compassionate God, all news is good news.

A baby will be born. He will be the answer to the promise made to Israel. He is the answer to our salvation. Miracles will happen.

The cup before us is also a miracle—a miracle of love and life eternal in Jesus Christ. We praise you, God, as we drink from this cup. Holy Spirit, guide us into paths where we may proclaim your good news to others. Amen.

UNIFIED PRAYER: We are a fortunate people indeed, God. You have shared with us that which is most important to you—your Son. By his life, death, and resurrection, you give us the good news of life eternal in your love. The loaf and cup before us tell of this love each time we come to the table. By the eating and drinking of the bread and wine, we commit ourselves to sharing what you have so freely given to us. Help us, Holy Spirit, to act in the name of our Savior, who comes again to us. Amen.*

STATEMENT AFTER COMMUNION: God is saying to us that in Jesus Christ, God is with each of us. Emmanuel, God with us. We believe the promise of God. Go! Share the good news!

---

*Dixon, *Everlasting Light,* p. 20.

Fourth Sunday of Advent

Isaiah 7:10–16
Psalm 80:1–7, 17–19
Romans 1:1–7
Matthew 1:18–25

PRAYER FOR THE BREAD: Savior God, we wait for your coming during this Advent season. We know the time is now near. Help us take the words of scripture we have heard in these weeks to reflect on a new way to live our lives, confess our sins, and wait in faith and hope for the coming of our Lord, Emmanuel.

Give us the courage to act for good and not for evil, hold us by the hand, and lead us in your paths.

We know the bread we take is for the forgiveness of our sins; we eat of it cleansed of what is not acceptable to you. We offer to you thanksgiving for our Savior. Holy Spirit, be with us we pray. Amen.

PRAYER FOR THE CUP: The psalmist cried, "Restore us, O LORD God of hosts; let your face shine, that we may be saved."* We anticipate your coming, Immanuel, knowing that we have the power to be saved if we but ask. We confess your name, O Jesus, and know we belong to you.

The cup is truly the symbol that we are saved, for it is the blood of our Savior. Increase our faith, and let our hope reign in this season of waiting for the coming of the one we call Christ. Amen.

*Psalm 80:19.

UNIFIED PRAYER: O God who is ever near us, in these final days before your coming, we offer our prayers to you. We thank you for life itself; we thank you for our church family. Most of all, we give you thanks for your Son, our Savior, Jesus Christ. In this meal today, we eat and drink in anticipation of the coming of the Christ. Help us to feel your presence, Emmanuel, God with us, as we take the bread and cup. Amen.*

STATEMENT AFTER COMMUNION:
Go as risk-takers,
for God has nourished you with bread and cup.
Go as new creatures,
for God is saving you from your sin.
Go as children of God,
for God will be with us all. Amen.**

*Sandy Dixon, *Everlasting Light,* p. 23.
**Diana Hagewood Smith, in McKiernan-Allen, ed., *Celebrating Incarnation,* p. 69.

Christmas Eve/Day

Isaiah 9:2–7	*Isaiah 62:6–12*	*Isaiah 52:7–10*
Psalm 96	*Psalm 97*	*Psalm 98*
Titus 2:11–14	*Titus 3:4–7*	*Hebrews 1:1–4, (5–12)*
Luke 2:1–14,	*Luke 2:(1–7),*	*John 1:1–14*
(15–20)	*8–20*	

(Any of the above scriptures may be used
on Christmas Eve or Christmas Day.)

PRAYER FOR THE BREAD: How wonderful are your ways, O God of light. Through your word, you have created far-flung galaxies, and through your word you came to us in Jesus the Christ. Today we celebrate Christ's coming and how he brought light into a world of darkness. Here, at this table, we witness to the fact that Christ took on human flesh and that he came to be the bread of the world. As you have blessed us with the Christ, we know that you will bless us as we eat this bread. May your Spirit open our eyes to the Jesus who was born in Bethlehem, and to the Christ who is in our midst today. Amen.

PRAYER FOR THE CUP: God of history, for many generations you spoke to your people through the prophets. Yet it is when you came to us in your very Son that we truly realized the great love you have for us. It is through your Son, Jesus Christ, that we see you. Through his teachings we know how to act according to your will.

We are awed by the totality of your love when we realize that your Son, whose birthday we are celebrating

CHRISTMAS

this evening (today), died for each of us. The cup on this table is the cup of your commitment to your people.

Holy Spirit, join us as we drink this cup of good news to all people. Amen.

UNIFIED PRAYER: We thank you, loving God, for Jesus, who came long ago as your beloved Child and who has come again in this feast of joy to be our light, our hope, our life. As we receive strength and spiritual nourishment from the bread and cup, let us be bearers of the everlasting light, messengers of eternal hope, and witnesses to new life in you. Amen.*

PRAYER AFTER COMMUNION: God of light, your presence has been with us as we have worshiped together. Your abundant love is evident as we celebrate the birth of the Christ Child, our Savior. We give you thanks that we are your people, coming together around this holy table. Amen.

*Dixon, *Everlasting Light,* p. 26, adapted from *Thankful Praise* (St. Louis: Chalice Press, 1987), p. 74.

First Sunday after Christmas

Isaiah 63:7–9
Psalm 148
Hebrews 2:10–18
Matthew 2:13–23

PRAYER FOR THE BREAD: This week we have celebrated the birth of our Savior. Great God of love, help us realize that this celebration was truly Emmanuel—God with us in the baby Jesus. You came to us as a child, a person, a Savior. You didn't send a message, a fax, or an e-mail with your news of salvation. You sent your only Son out of your great love for us.

This bread on the table before us is a sign of your presence continuing with us. We are assured that, as we eat this bread, we are redeemed in your great love. Your glory is above earth and heaven! Praise the Lord! Amen.

PRAYER FOR THE CUP: We live in a world where terrible things happen. There are natural disasters, terminal illnesses, famine, war, death of innocent children and of adults. Your people suffer, merciful God. Yet in our suffering we are aware of your mercy, presence, and love. Your only Son suffered and died. Our Savior was also aware of your great love that we see in the resurrection.

We know that in an imperfect world there can be suffering. But we are promised that your presence will be with us always in Emmanuel. This cup of suffering has been transformed into a cup of joy and praise.

We drink from this cup, transformed into new life of hope made flesh. Amen.

UNIFIED PRAYER: O Creator of love and life, we come to this table today full of the joy of Christmas. We are confident that your love and presence will not be put away like the bright decorations. We are confident that your gift to us, your Son and our Savior, will not be seasonal, going away when the holiday is over. This bread and cup are always here before us, as is your great love. We know this presence through your Son, Emmanuel, God with us. We feel your presence in the Holy Spirit as we eat and drink together in your name. Amen.[*]

PRAYER AFTER COMMUNION: "The truth of Christmas lingers on. Just when we are ready to give up, the sheer power of God's love breaks through again. God is with us! Do not be afraid!"[**] The bread and cup, the body and blood of our Savior—praise be to God! Amen.

[*]Dixon, *Everlasting Light,* p. 29.
[**]J. Phillip Wogaman, in *The Upper Room Disciplines 1998,* ed. Rita Collett (Nashville: Upper Room, 1997), p. 69.

Second Sunday after Christmas

Jeremiah 31:7–14
Psalm 147:12–20
Ephesians 1:3–14
John 1:(1–9), 10–18

PRAYER FOR THE BREAD: O God of time eternal, as we face the transition from one year to another, we come to this table in an attitude of confession. We have strayed from our resolutions and promises. The good that we had intended was not all done; in fact, we may have done some evil. With good intention, we nevertheless have let ourselves stray. We, like the Israelites, are exiled from our hopes and distanced from our goals.[*]

Yet it is at this table that our hope in God comes full circle and we can ask for forgiveness. The bread of forgiveness is for all God's people. In the sharing of this bread, we celebrate the Christ who was born, lived, died, and lives eternally.

Help us, Holy Spirit, so that in the breaking and eating of this bread, we will have new vision for our lives in this new year. Amen.

PRAYER FOR THE CUP: God of grace, whose incomprehensible love for us is revealed at this table, we offer you praise and thanksgiving. In your great wisdom, you sent us your own Son so that we may know you. Through his life, teachings, death, and resurrection, you showed us the way of life itself.

This cup shows your commitment to give light to us who walk in darkness. The light is our Savior, Jesus Christ,

[*]Justo Gonzales, in The *Upper Room Disciplines 1996,* ed. Glenda Webb (Nashville: Upper Room, 1995), p. 379.

who gave his life for us. In the drinking of this cup, we can walk in the light.

Holy Spirit, help us become a light to those whose paths are in darkness; help us, as you did John the Baptist, point to the Christ. Amen.

UNIFIED PRAYER: In joyful praise we come to the table this day, O God and Father of our Lord, Jesus Christ. We offer thanksgiving for all that you have done for us. You have chosen us to be your people, adopted us into your holy family through Jesus Christ. In Christ Jesus, we experience redemption, forgiveness, and grace.

Yet at this table, we experience even a more abundant gift from you. Through this bread and cup, the giving of Jesus Christ himself, we are the recipients of life eternal!

We have celebrated the birth of our Savior; we have celebrated the giving of your Son; we celebrate your plan for the fullness of time. We pray that you will reveal your will for us in this year to come. Amen.

PRAYER AFTER COMMUNION:
"O thou joyful, O thou wonderful grace revealing
Christmastide!
Jesus came to win us from all sin within us;
glorify the holy child.
O thou joyful, O thou wonderful love revealing
Christmastide!
Loud hosannas singing and all praises bringing:
may Thy love with us abide!"* Amen.

*Johannes D. Falk, "O Thou Joyful," trans. Henry Katterjohn (1919).

Epiphany

Isaiah 60:1–6
Psalm 72:1–7, 10–14
Ephesians 3:1–12
Matthew 2:1–12

PRAYER FOR THE BREAD:
"Come Blessed Bread
We are hungry.
Nourish us with your presence
strengthen us to serve
enable us to forgive
inspire us to pray
and encourage us to share
the feast of your love,
a banquet for all."* Amen.

PRAYER FOR THE CUP: On this festive day, we celebrate the message that you had planned for us—that Christ came for all people. You did not forget your people in bondage; you rescued them and restored them as your people. We praise you. You sent your Son, Jesus Christ for all. For those who came to seek Jesus from far away, we praise you. You gave us the gift of your Son so that we may live eternally with you. We praise you. We drink together from this cup that reminds us of this wonderful plan you have for us. We praise you. Amen.

*Janice K. Stanton, *The Secret Place,* Fall 1999 (American Baptist Churches in the U.S.A. Educational Ministries): p. 29.

UNIFIED PRAYER: Creator of Heaven and Earth, you have revealed yourself in your Son, Jesus Christ, our light and salvation. "You sent a star to guide the Magi to where the Christ was born; and your signs and witnesses in every age and through all the world have led your people from far places to his light."* On this day of Epiphany, we celebrate the coming of those who sought a Savior.

In eating this bread and drinking from this cup, we celebrate that we know a Savior, Jesus Christ. In the presence of the Holy Spirit, let us commune in the light of the Word. Amen.

PRAYER AFTER COMMUNION: Gracious God, here at this table we have been in the company of Jesus Christ, our Savior and Redeemer. You have revealed your loving ways to us in broken bread and poured cup. Now as your light has illuminated our lives, help us be a light for others. Amen.

---

*Hoyt Hickman et al., *The New Handbook of the Christian Year* (Nashville, Abingdon Press, 1992), p. 86f.

First Sunday after Epiphany

Isaiah 42:1–9
Psalm 29
Acts 10:34–43
Matthew 3:13–17

PRAYER FOR THE BREAD: You have given us a message of peace, gracious God, and called us to proclaim it. Once we were outsiders, and you have blessed and accepted us. Once we were lost, and your light has come upon us to show us the way. In eating this bread, we accept your covenant and remember the Christ who gave his own life for us. Through your Spirit, help us see the signs of your blessing and love that are scattered throughout our daily lives. Through your Spirit, help us be sources of blessing and givers of your love to those around us. Amen.

PRAYER FOR THE CUP: To fulfill all righteousness, your Son, Jesus Christ was baptized, dear God. To show us your way, Jesus Christ walked humbly and lightly in our midst, teaching, healing, and helping those who had been bruised and battered in life. He was willing to drink of the cup of suffering so that we might drink of the cup of life. As we drink this cup of life, help us remember our own baptism. Help us realize how we have been called through death to life. You have shown us your path, O loving God. May your Spirit descend upon us, bless us, and help us stay true to your way. Amen.

UNIFIED PRAYER: In the violence of a storm, we experience your power, majestic God. In the flash of lightning we see your glory. In the peace of a starry night, in every breath we take, we discover your creative energy and the awesome beauty of your holiness. Yet you care for us. You call us to be a covenant people. You challenge us to do the work of our Savior in bringing light to the nations, sight to the blind, freedom to the prisoner. And in Jesus Christ, you have given us an example to follow. In Jesus Christ, you have revealed your redeeming love. The bread we eat and the cup from which we drink help us recall the Christ who is here with us now; they help us see the human face of your tender love. Empower us by your Spirit so that others may see in us the love of Jesus Christ and so that we might be a blessing to them. Amen.

PRAYER AFTER COMMUNION: We are people of the good news. We are people who have received a great and wonderful gift. We are people on whom the light has shined. We are people who have been to God's table. Hallelujah! Amen.

Second Sunday after Epiphany

Isaiah 49:1–7
Psalm 40:1–11
1 Corinthians 1:1–9
John 1:29–42

PRAYER FOR THE BREAD: You have put a new song in our hearts, merciful God, a song of freedom, of hope, and of praise. You have lifted us from despair and set us upon the rock of faith. Here at this communion table, we stand upon that firm foundation, the love of our Lord Jesus Christ. As we break bread, we remember that love. As we eat this bread, we feed on that love. May that love sustain us and work through us as we try to live as Christians in the week ahead. Guide us by your Spirit, that we may be faithful to you. Amen.

PRAYER FOR THE CUP: You are faithful, eternal God. Your love never fails. Help us learn to trust your love, to accept the gift of your Son, Jesus Christ. Enlighten us with your light, so that we may see Jesus as the one who came to take away the sins of the world. In this cup that we now lift, we remember that Christ's blood was shed for the forgiveness of sins. Help us live forgiven lives, and help us forgive others, by your Spirit's guidance. Amen.

UNIFIED PRAYER: You have given us a testimony through prophecy and scriptures, faithful God, that we might recognize the Christ. You have called us to be your disciples, wise God, that we might learn your will and your way for our lives. You have given us this table, compassionate God, that we might find here the strength and refreshment that we need to live as your servants. Bless us as we eat this bread, and help us remember that Christ came to be our living bread. Bless us as we drink this cup, and help us remember that Christ is the living water. Through your Spirit, may we ever be aware that we are yours, and that you are the source of all that is good. May we feed on your love and feed others with your love throughout this week. Amen.

STATEMENT AFTER COMMUNION: We gathered at the table, called here by the Lamb of God. We have shared together the bread and the cup, and have dined as Christ's guests. Let us go from this place satisfied and refreshed, living in the spirit of the one who goes before us.

Third Sunday after Epiphany

Isaiah 9:1–4
Psalm 27:1, 4–9
1 Corinthians 1:10–18
Matthew 4:12–23

PRAYER FOR THE BREAD: Wonderful counselor, we come to this table drawn by the light of your love. Here we reflect upon the cross of Jesus and find a wisdom that the world thinks of as foolishness, a power that the world thinks of as weakness. Here we eat a tiny piece of bread and call it a banquet, all because it reminds us of the one who died so that we might have life. Nourish us with this bread; let it satisfy our souls. Hear us as we pray with the Spirit's power in the name of the good teacher. Amen.

PRAYER FOR THE CUP: Mighty God, you are our light and salvation; whom shall we fear? You are our strength and security; why should we be afraid? We offer our fears and anxieties to you as we come to the table, knowing that you will accept them as you accept us, with grace and compassion. The cup that we now drink serves as a reminder that Christ's love for each of us is eternal and that you never give up on your children. You protect us and shelter us in all the storms of life so that we might sing your praises forever. Strengthen us in your Spirit. Amen.

UNIFIED PRAYER: Everlasting Father, Eternal Mother, when we follow our own ways, we end up stumbling in the darkness of fear and frustration, sin and alienation. Yet you allow us to see your light and to follow it, and in following it, we find Christ. What good news! We have been invited to be a part of your reign, to be agents of your love and justice, to be witnesses to your truth and light. We gather now at your table, to pledge ourselves to you in love and devotion because we have seen your beauty. For here we remember the beauty of Jesus' blessing and sharing the bread and the cup with his disciples. Bless us now as we partake, and dedicate us to be your people, led by your Spirit. Amen.

PRAYER AFTER COMMUNION: Prince of Peace, here we have sung your praises, here we have seen your face in the face of Jesus Christ, here we have shared in a special meal in your name. Help us go forth singing, not being afraid to praise you and to proclaim the good news of your reign. Amen.

Fourth Sunday after Epiphany

Micah 6:1–8
Psalm 15
1 Corinthians 1:18–31
Matthew 5:1–12

PRAYER FOR THE BREAD: O God of wisdom, what we do here does not make sense by the standards of this world. We come to worship one whom the world might call a loser, one who died a criminal's death in shame and disgrace. Yet before that death on a cross, Jesus Christ gathered his followers, broke bread with them, and shared of himself. After that death, he rose in glory, and his spirit is with us today, proving that your foolishness is wiser than human wisdom, your weakness stronger than human strength. In eating this bread, we acknowledge your way as the way for our lives. Bless us in your unconquerable love, given to us in Jesus Christ our Savior. Amen.

PRAYER FOR THE CUP: God of love and mercy, if we had to sacrifice to win your love, what would be enough? What could we give that could possibly overcome the division of sin, the barriers of selfishness that separate us?

"Were the whole realm of nature mine, that were a present far too small; love so amazing, so divine, demands my soul, my life, my all."*

Yet we realize, O God, that we don't have to make the sacrifice to win your love, for you have made the sacrifice through Jesus Christ. In drinking this cup, we honor that sacrifice and receive him into our lives, to

*Isaac Watts, "When I Survey the Wondrous Cross" (1707).

renew them and reshape them through your Spirit to your glory. Amen.

UNIFIED PRAYER: In a world that applauds arrogance, you call us to be meek. In a world that rewards competitiveness, you call us to kindness. In a world that teaches us to be aggressive, you call us to be peacemakers. At first, that may seem to be an impossible burden, dear God. But then we see the face of Christ and realize that instead you have given us a blessing, and called us to be a blessing. Here at this table we seek to redefine ourselves, our lives, and our values, that we might be more like Christ. As we eat this bread, we remember Christ's willingness to give of himself. As we drink from this cup, we remember Christ's love poured out for us. Strengthen us, nourish us, and guide us by your Spirit as we gather to remember what Christ has given for us. Amen.

STATEMENT AFTER COMMUNION: Here we have been challenged. Here we have been strengthened. Here we have been fed. With God's Spirit as our guide, may we go into the world to do justice, love kindness, and walk humbly with our God.

Fifth Sunday after Epiphany

Isaiah 58:1–9a, (9b–12)
Psalm 112:1–9 (10)
1 Corinthians 2:1–12, (13–16)
Matthew 5:13–20

PRAYER FOR THE BREAD: Great teacher, we come as students, eager to follow your way. Help us find the wisdom we seek, so that we may make sense of our lives. Here at this table, we learn that Jesus was always willing to share what he had with those in need. As Jesus shared bread with the disciples and with the hungry crowds, teach us to share bread with the hungry around us. We pray also that you will teach us to admit our own needs and hungers, so that we may find true satisfaction in the bread that we eat. Through your Spirit, help us learn that the secret of wisdom is the secret of compassion. Amen.

PRAYER FOR THE CUP: Light of the world, we seek to be lights to the world. We come to drink of this cup in an act that has rich meaning to us. Yet if we do not learn here to love and care for other people as Christ loved and cared for us, our ritual is empty, and our worship meaningless. For the cup we drink is the love of Christ, poured out for many, not just for us. Help us realize that if we are to be vessels of your love, our love too must pour out for others. Through your Spirit, may we understand and use the wonderful gifts that you have given us, so that we may truly be lights to the world. Amen.

Unified Prayer: In coming to this table, O God of light, we come seeking a way out of our own darkness, the darkness of sin and selfishness. Here we see Christ's love shine forth as the sun shines forth at dawn. Here our gracious host blesses the bread and pours the cup, demonstrating to us that your love shall never die. Here we witness to the power of Christ crucified, the glory of Christ risen from the dead, and the presence of the living Christ in our midst. May these realities work within our hearts as we digest these elements, reshaping our lives so that others may see the risen Christ in our love, our words, our service, and our compassion. Guide us by your Spirit's light so that we may be lights to the world. Amen.

Statement after Communion: Here, through the guidance of the Spirit, we have received a demonstration of God's love. We have experienced at this table the goodness of God and the love of Christ. Now may that same Spirit search our spirits and nurture them, so that we may reflect in our lives the goodness of God and the love of Christ.

Sixth Sunday after Epiphany (Proper 1)

Deuteronomy 30:15–20
Psalm 119:1–8
1 Corinthians 3:1–9
Matthew 5:21–37

PRAYER FOR THE BREAD: We pray to you, O Teacher God, because you have sent us Jesus Christ so that we might learn your ways. You know that like children, we learn by imitation, and you have given us this table as a place of learning. Here, as we break bread, we imitate Jesus Christ breaking bread, so that we might learn that Jesus is the bread of life. Help us learn to imitate Christ not only in breaking bread but also in loving one another, in giving of ourselves to one another, and in living out the good news of your love. May your Spirit instruct us when we need to learn, pick us up when we stumble, and open our hearts to see Christ in others around us. Amen.

PRAYER FOR THE CUP: We gather at this table, merciful God, realizing that this cup is a strong symbol of your forgiveness and your desire to restore us to relationship with you and with one another. Often we are like the disciples in the upper room, weak and anxious, struggling with doubts, fears, and even betrayal. As this cup is passed, open our hearts to the power of your forgiveness. Through your Spirit's power, help us find here the strength to live gently and lovingly. We pray in the name of the one who sealed with this cup your covenant of love and mercy. Amen.

UNIFIED PRAYER: God of all people, you have created us so that we need one another to survive. You have given us law and leadership, so that we might build community. Through Jesus Christ, you have reminded us that when we have wronged one another, we must become reconciled with our brother or sister before coming to your altar, for love of God and love of neighbor are one. Forgive us, dear God, for the pain that we have caused one another, and give us the ability to forgive others and to receive forgiveness. May the bread that we now eat and the cup that we now pour remind us of the Christ you sent to show us the ways of forgiveness, the paths of peace. In taking these emblems, bless us by your Spirit, so that we may learn to live as you would want us to live. Amen.

PRAYER AFTER COMMUNION: You have shown us the path of life, compassionate God. At this table, we have received a lesson in what it is to be your loving people. As we go, help us be responsive to your Spirit's guiding. Amen.

Seventh Sunday after Epiphany (Proper 2)

Leviticus 19:1–2, 9–18
Psalm 119:33–40
1 Corinthians 3:10–11, 16–23
Matthew 5:38–48

PRAYER FOR THE BREAD: We come to your table, dear God, because through the living Christ you have invited us. We have come to learn, to discern your will for us as individuals and as a congregation. We have come to pray, to listen to the guidance of your Spirit. We have come to break bread, to follow the instructions of our Lord Jesus Christ, who called us to share this loaf and to remember him. Bless this bread and bless our lives by your Spirit, and guide us as we walk the paths of discipleship. Amen.

PRAYER FOR THE CUP: Holy God, you have called us to be a holy people, to live lives of forgiveness and mercy. Yet we struggle with acting holy, forgiving, or merciful. We thank you for sending us Jesus Christ to teach us your way and to bring us new life. Now, gathered at the table that you have spread, we come to drink of the cup that reminds us of Christ's love poured out for us. Bless us as we drink, so that we may feel the power of the risen Christ in our lives, transforming us by your Spirit. Amen.

UNIFIED PRAYER: Teach us your way, dear God. Guide us on the path of love and loyalty. We become so distracted by the pressures of daily life and by the desire to accumulate worldly treasures that we often ignore the love that formed us. Here at this table, may this time of silence and reflection be a time of learning for us, a time of reevaluation, a time of sorting. Here at this table, we remember the way of love for God and neighbor that Christ taught us. Here at this table, in the act of sharing bread and wine, we honor the Christ who gave his life that we might live. As these elements we consume become part of our bodies, may the living Christ become part of our hearts, minds, and spirits. Bless us by your Spirit, in Christ's name. Amen.

PRAYER AFTER COMMUNION: Gracious God, you have called us together to worship you. You have heard our prayers. You have given us this table, where we have received bread and drink and remembered our Lord Jesus Christ. But you have not asked that we stay in this holy place. You have called us back into the world and promised through Christ that you would be with us always. Thank you, God, for this mission and this promise. Amen.

Eighth Sunday after Epiphany (Proper 3)

Isaiah 49:8–16a
Psalm 131
1 Corinthians 4:1–5
Matthew 6:24–34

PRAYER FOR THE BREAD: How wonderful is your love, God of all mercy. What an amazing thing it is that you care for us, that you know us as individuals, that you seek what is best for us. When we get trapped in sin, feeling as if we are in exile from your presence, you come to bring us home, so that we might rejoice in your forgiveness. When we come home, we find that you have set a table for us. Here we find nourishment for our souls as we eat the bread you offer. Here we remember Christ's giving of himself to show us the way of your love. As we eat this bread, surround us with your Spirit, so that we might live as your faithful, loving children. Amen.

PRAYER FOR THE CUP: As we come to this table, gracious God, we feel humbled that you have invited us to be stewards of your mystery. Here we reenact Christ's meal with his disciples and ponder your overwhelming gift of love for your children. We pray that we may not take this meal, or your love, lightly, not expecting anything to happen. Instead, touch us at the depths of our hearts, so that we may realize the power of your love. In drinking this cup, we remember Christ's sacrifice, how his life was poured out for us. Bless us with the gift of your Spirit as we drink it, so we might be worthy of your trust. Amen.

UNIFIED PRAYER: Calm our souls, God of peace. Quiet our spirits. Surround us with your love so we feel as secure in it as a baby feels in the love of its mother. Fill us with the realization that your love never abandons us. Help us find freedom from the worries and fears that imprison us. Give us the understanding that this table is a symbol of your steadfast love, of your constant care for your children. Here we can offer up our worries about earthly things, turn them over to you, and receive your peace. We come now to break bread and to drink wine, thereby remembering Christ's sacrifice for us. Bless us as we partake, so that we might know Christ's presence here with us. Send us your Spirit, that through it we might know more fully the amazing power of your love. Amen.

STATEMENT AFTER COMMUNION: Here at this table, we have affirmed God's faithfulness and love, and have opened our lives to the transforming power of God's spirit. We go from this place in trust and joy, knowing that God will never, no, never, no, never forsake us.

Last Sunday after Epiphany

Exodus 24:12–18
Psalm 2 or *Psalm 99*
2 Peter 1:16–21
Matthew 17:1–9

PRAYER FOR THE BREAD: God of clouds and smoke, God of light and flame, God of the quiet place and the inner voice, we come to you in love, awe, and gratitude. As you have revealed yourself so dramatically to your children in the Bible, you reveal yourself to us here in a quieter way, at this table. Here we see your forgiving, caring, and loving nature as we come and break bread. This bread is fragile and breaks easily. We are fragile and break easily. Through Jesus Christ, you took on our fragility and weakness for our sake and gave us the hope of resurrection glory. Through your spirit, may we learn to appreciate this wonderful gift and to share it with others. Amen.

PRAYER FOR THE CUP: How wonderful it must have been on the mountain, God of mystery. How wonderful and awesome it must have been to see that glowing cloud, to see Moses, Elijah, and your own Son, Jesus Christ, in a glowing white garment, and to hear you bless him as your Beloved. Yet where we are is wonderful and awesome too. Here we share in a mystery, the mystery of your love poured out for us in the death and resurrection of Christ. Through your Spirit, bless this cup as we pour and drink from it, that our eyes might be opened to the wonders of your love. Amen.

UNIFIED PRAYER: God of glory, we come into your presence with awe and wonder. You are awesome and frightening, like a flame or light too bright for our eyes. We can't behold your glory directly. You appeared in holy light on Mount Sinai to give your law to your people. You appeared in holy light on another mountain to give Jesus Christ your blessing and seal. We praise your great and awesome name. How wonderful it is that through Jesus Christ, we can know you personally. In the act of sharing bread and wine, we can be in communion with the living Christ and with you. Bless now the bread we break, in Christ's name. Bless now the cup we pour, in Christ's name. Bless us as we eat and drink, in Christ's name, for he is your beloved son, and through him we are all your beloved children. May your Spirit open our spirits, so that we may learn what you would teach us. Amen.

PRAYER AFTER COMMUNION: God, you are the holy One. We thank you for these moments of communion together with your Son, your Beloved, Jesus Christ. As we go from this table, let us realize that we never leave your holy presence, that every place can be a holy mountain, for you are there. Amen.

First Sunday in Lent

Genesis 2:15–17; 3:1–7
Psalm 32
Romans 5:12–19
Matthew 4:1–11

PRAYER FOR THE BREAD: Creator God, you have created a pure world, and we have turned it into a toxic world. So much around us that seems attractive and appealing is destructive and dangerous in the long run. Help us past the temptation to eat spiritual junk food. Help us realize that where we are now gathered, we are offered the bread of life. In this Lenten season, we realize how precious this bread is. Give us the grace to take and eat it, and to share it with others. Through it, may we be bound together by your Holy Spirit. Amen.

PRAYER FOR THE CUP: You are the God of redeeming love. Hear us as we pray. So often we are afraid to admit to ourselves that we are a sinful, broken people. We want to cover the blemishes of our lack of love, and hope that you won't see them. We rationalize and make excuses. Help us to trust in your goodness, which redeems rather than judges. Help us to be willing to listen to your words of instruction and your words of forgiveness. We lift before you the cup, remembering that it is a cup of forgiveness. We remember as we drink it that Jesus shed his blood so that we might be forgiven. Deliver us by the power of your Spirit to the new life we seek, as free and forgiven people. Amen.

UNIFIED PRAYER: Although we live in a comfortable, high-tech society, Holy God, we sometimes experience life as a wilderness. Threats and temptations are on every side. We feel lost and in need of guidance, but in our insecurity, we seek the quick fix, the easy way out. As we gather at this table, help us remember that we are not alone in temptation, that even Jesus was tempted. Help us realize that in Jesus we can find strength to overcome, and forgiveness when we do not. We gather at this table today remembering that Jesus turned down unholy bread, the bread of selfishness, but that Jesus lifted up holy bread, the bread of self-sacrificing love. We gather at this table knowing that Jesus turned down the wine of earthly splendor but that he lifted up the cup of sacrifice and love. May we be true to our Savior as we eat and drink. May we be quick to follow your Spirit through our wilderness to your presence. Amen.

PRAYER AFTER COMMUNION: We part from Christ's table, knowing that in Jesus Christ we have been justified, in Jesus Christ we have been redeemed, in Jesus Christ we have been forgiven. Now, dear God, help us live our daily lives as if we were truly justified, redeemed, and forgiven. Amen.

Second Sunday in Lent

Genesis 12:1–4a
Psalm 121
Romans 4:1–5, 13–17
John 3:1–17 or *Matthew 17:1–9*

PRAYER FOR THE BREAD: You, God, are our help; your love neither falters nor fails. You, God, keep us and protect us; you preserve us from evil. We trust you because you have given us Jesus Christ, your beloved Son, who put aside his glory that we might have life. We thank you for this gift of bread, through which we recall your gift of Christ's physical presence on earth. As we eat from this loaf, help us to have the faith to accept the living Christ's presence in our lives here and now. Guide us and bless us by your Spirit. Amen.

PRAYER FOR THE CUP: We come to this table, God of new life, as cautious as Nicodemus, not knowing what to expect and not always sure that we really want what you have to give. As we come to this table to drink from the cup, symbolizing the life of Christ poured out for us, help us overcome our fears and hesitation to accept the free gift of life that you offer. Help us realize in awe and wonder that you loved each one of us enough to send your Son. May your Spirit, which moves as mysteriously as the wind blows, move within us and among us to bring us new life in Christ Jesus. Amen.

UNIFIED PRAYER: God of all ages, you sometimes call us from places of comfort and security to risky journeys of faith. We are often afraid to follow, unwilling to risk changes in our lives, even though we know that you are the source of all life. Help us be like Abraham, able to put aside that which holds us back, so that we might follow you freely. In this Lenten season, we recognize that this table is a symbol that wherever we are on our faith journeys, you are there. You sustain us by the bread that we break and the cup that we pour. In these elements we remember the Christ—transfigured, suffering, dying, risen, and in our midst today. May your Spirit be our guide as we walk in new paths of faith. Amen.

PRAYER AFTER COMMUNION: Ever-living and ever-loving God, we can only begin to comprehend your glory, your power, your love, and your compassion. We have come to this table to learn something of this mystery. As we go from this table, may we follow you faithfully as your disciples. Amen.

Third Sunday in Lent

Exodus 17:1–7
Psalm 95
Romans 5:1–11
John 4:5–42

PRAYER FOR THE BREAD: Creator God, we sing your praise because all creation is in your hands. Shepherd God, we sing your praise because you care for us and feed us. We are the people of your pasture, the sheep of your hand. In Jesus Christ, you meet our deepest needs. In him, our souls are fed. We thank you for this bread, for it reminds us that Christ gave of himself that our spirits might be sustained. Lead us by your Spirit that we might be your faithful people. Amen.

PRAYER FOR THE CUP: God of life and power, all life springs from you. When your children cried out from thirst in the desert, you gave them water from the rock. When Jesus met the woman at the well, he offered her living water, the water of your grace that sustains all life. We too come seeking the living water. We too come to this table to be refreshed and restored. As we drink from this cup, help us realize that it is Christ who sustains and refreshes us, that it is Christ who gives us life. May your Spirit be poured out on us, so that we may know what it is to truly live. Amen.

UNIFIED PRAYER: God of glory, God of love, in your presence we find peace and wholeness. You have come to us in Jesus Christ, and proved your love for us at the cross. At the cross, we have been justified, we have been reconciled, and we have been forgiven. Yet at this table, we remember not only that Christ suffered and died for us but that Christ conquered death. We are not drawn here by the dead Jesus whom we remember, but by the living Christ whom we experience. Bless us as we eat this bread, for in so doing we remember that your love took on human flesh. Bless us as we drink this cup, for in so doing, we remember that your love has been poured into our hearts through the Holy Spirit. May this love transform our relationships, renew our congregation, and strengthen our witness to you in the daily world. Amen.

STATEMENT AFTER COMMUNION: We have obtained access to the grace of God through Jesus Christ. At this table, we have celebrated and symbolized this love and have experienced the presence of the risen Christ. Through Christ, we have been reconciled to God. Let us go into the world and be reconciled to one another in Christ's name.

Fourth Sunday in Lent

1 Samuel 16:1–13
Psalm 23
Ephesians 5:8–14
John 9:1–41

PRAYER FOR THE BREAD: God of light, you have called us to be children of the light. In Jesus Christ we have received the light of your love, the light that can guide us in the ways of peace, justice, and truth. In breaking this bread, we remember that Jesus Christ offered his own life so that our lives might be lived in resurrection glory. Help us by the power of your Spirit to walk in the light of your love. Amen.

PRAYER FOR THE CUP: In our lives, dear God, we are sometimes frightened by dark and dangerous times. Sometimes we are caught up in fear and depression. We find ourselves walking in the valley of the shadow. We gather now as did Christ and the disciples in the upper room, knowing that even in the darkest times you are with us, guiding us and comforting us. This wine we drink is a reminder of the covenant sealed in that upper room, a reminder that Christ walks with us today. By your Spirit's grace, help us realize that we are never alone. Amen.

UNIFIED PRAYER: God of light and love, you have sent us your Son, Jesus Christ, to be the light of the world. We remember the Christ who brought light, hope, and healing into the lives of many. We remember that through your amazing grace, Christ brought sight to the eyes of a young man born blind and called his followers to work for the light. We remember the time that Christ gathered at a table with his disciples, in a dark room, in a dark time. We remember how he blessed and broke the bread, how he blessed and poured the cup, and in so doing, gave them a love stronger than death. This love has called us to this table today, and by your Spirit's power we are still bound by that love. Help us to walk in the light of your love. Amen.

PRAYER AFTER COMMUNION: Gracious God, you have not called us to this table because we are strong, good, or deserving. You have set this table before us and invited us here because you love us, even in our unworthiness. We pray that your grace may work through our lives in the days ahead, so that we may glorify and praise you. Amen.

Fifth Sunday in Lent

Ezekiel 37:1–14
Psalm 130
Romans 8:6–11
John 11:1–45

PRAYER FOR THE BREAD: You are the living God, and at your table we gather. When our lives feel dry and barren, your Spirit moves among us, and the dry bones of our spirits come to new life once more. Bless this bread that we break and eat in imitation of your Son, Jesus Christ, and the disciples. Through this act of obedience and remembrance, may we grow in discipleship, and in love for the savior who came and died to bring us new life. May your Spirit quicken us, so that we may receive and reflect the new life you offer. Amen.

PRAYER FOR THE CUP: If you, O God, held our sins and fears, our compromises and cowardice against us, who could stand? But you are a forgiving God. You hear us when we cry in the depths, lead us from the depths to a joyous place. We come to this table with eagerness and longing, realizing that it is a taste of the heavenly communion you promise us. This cup we drink reminds us of the cup of sorrow and suffering that Jesus drank, but it also reminds us of the wine of joy that we will share in glory. By your Spirit, may we realize that you are always with us, in the depths as well as the heights, in the darkness as well as the brightness of day. Amen.

UNIFIED PRAYER: God of new life, we gather in this community as your faithful people. In faith we proclaim with Mary and Martha that Jesus is the Messiah, your Son. In faith we hear him say that he is the resurrection and the life. In faith we gather at this table to remember his death, to celebrate his resurrection, and to affirm his presence. Bless the bread, and through it strengthen our spirits as bread strengthens our bodies. Bless the wine, and through it bring us the joy of knowing that you are near. And more, we pray you will bless us with the gift of your Spirit, that we may live each day as children of joy, peace, and new life. Amen.

PRAYER AFTER COMMUNION: We thank you, life-giving God, for all the ways that you can work within our lives to transform us into your faithful people. We thank you especially for this communion meal and for the time it has given us to reflect on your presence. We pray that we may go from this place refreshed and aware of your presence and love, not only here, but in every moment of every day. Amen.

Sixth Sunday in Lent (Palm Sunday)

Psalm 118:1–2, 19–29
Matthew 21:1–11*

PRAYER FOR THE BREAD: We praise you, God of righteousness, because you offer us the road of life. We praise you for sending Jesus Christ to show us the way to true life. Help us learn to trust you, to follow the Way. Give us joyous hearts to praise you and proclaim Christ as our ruler. In the bread we break, may we realize what it means to profess Christ as ruler of our lives. May we realize the cost of the love you have given us through Christ, so that we may respond as faithful and loyal disciples. When we would be fearful of following Christ, may your Spirit give us courage. Amen.

PRAYER FOR THE CUP: Hosanna, King Jesus, Hosanna. You are truly blessed, for you come to us in the name of God. Hosanna in the highest heaven. On that Palm Sunday long ago, you made a claim and a challenge to be the king of peace. As we gather here to drink this cup of communion, we accept for ourselves the claim and challenge that you made; we affirm the covenant that you offered. Bless us with your Spirit as we drink. Amen.

---

*These are the scriptures for the "Liturgy of the Palms," on which these prayers are based. The scriptures for the "Liturgy of the Passion" are: Isaiah 50:4–9a; Psalm 31:9–16; Philippians 2:5–11; and Matthew 26:14–27:66 *or* Matthew 27:11–54.

UNIFIED PRAYER: We give you thanks, O God, for you are good. Your steadfast love endures forever. As Jesus Christ entered the gates of Jerusalem long ago, he opened for us the gates of righteousness so that we might come into your presence. We are not a righteous people, but you have restored us to a right relationship with you through Christ's sacrifice on the cross. During this Holy Week, help us recall the story of our Savior's suffering, death, and resurrection. May the bread we offer and the cup we drink help our Savior's story live within our hearts and lives. As we participate in this holy meal, help us declare our allegiance to the one who comes in your name, Jesus Christ our Lord. May the Spirit guide us as we follow the one who comes in your name. Amen.

STATEMENT AFTER COMMUNION: Hosanna to God our creator! Hosanna to the one who God sent to rule over our lives, Jesus Christ. We go from this table, filled with love and praise, inspired by Christ's spirit, to carry the good news of Christ into our world, in word and deed.

Maundy Thursday

Exodus 12:1–4, (5–10), 11–14
Psalm 116:1–2, 12–19
1 Corinthians 11:23–26
John 13:1–17, 31b–35

PRAYER FOR THE BREAD: God, who gives life itself, on this night of remembrance we confess that we, like Judas, have faced temptations that lead us to betray Christ. Yet we know that we may eat from the bread of salvation. We know that this bread can point us in the direction of a Christlike life. Please forgive our sins.

On this, the darkest of all nights, help us to remember that just as the grain that made this bread grew from a seemingly lifeless seed into wheat, Christ rose from the dead into new life. Holy Spirit, help us feel the hope that keeps faith alive as we eat this loaf of salvation. Amen.

PRAYER FOR THE CUP: O God who is ever near, we come to the table on this holy night asking for your guidance and direction in our lives. We remember that on that special night, Jesus became a servant. He offered himself to the disciples, washing their feet, giving them an example of how to live the Christian life.

This cup of servanthood that we share can empower us to become the servants you truly want us to be. Let us drink from the cup and then go into the world, loving one another. Holy Spirit, give us faith and strength to say, "O Lord, I am your servant." Show us the way of the servant-filled Christian as our Lord taught us. Amen.

UNIFIED PRAYER: Our Great Shepherd, we observe today the simple ceremony you left us. With ordinary elements of bread and drink, we remember that night in which you, the Great Shepherd, became the slain Lamb of sacrifice.

Through this familiar ritual in which we find hope, we remember the night that you left the comfort of ritual and familiarity to enter the chaos of the unknown.

You left the well-lit upper room and the safety of friends to enter the darkness that would overcome the Light. And ultimately you set aside your power and laid down your life to give us the gift of eternal life.

Before celebrating the glorious end of the night, through partaking of these elements, we your church would confess that we have at times not loved as deeply as we should in receiving the stranger among us, in honoring the humble, in visiting the poor, in speaking justice on behalf of the oppressed.

Forgive us, for we confess, "Worthy is the Lamb, that was slain to receive power and riches, wisdom and strength, honor and glory and praise." Amen.[*]

PRAYER AFTER COMMUNION:
"Love beyond all comprehension,
offered through this feast divine,
we can only go in joy
to share with all our bread and wine."[**] Amen.

---

[*]Israel Galindo, *Let Us Pray* (Judson Press, 1999), p. 77.
[**]Peter Olejar, "Now We Come Before God's Presence" (1992), © 1995 Chalice Press.

Easter Day

Acts 10:34–43 or *Jeremiah 31:1–6*
Psalm 118:1–2, 14–24
Colossians 3:1–4 or *Acts 10:34–43*
John 20:1–18 or *Matthew 28:1–10*

PRAYER FOR THE BREAD: (based on Psalm 118) "O Give thanks to the Lord, for he is good; his steadfastness endures forever!" At this table we know that the Lord did not die, but lives. The bread that is on the table before us is truly Living Bread! "This is the Lord's doing; it is marvelous in our eyes. This is the day that the Lord has made; let us rejoice and be glad in it." Amen.

PRAYER FOR THE CUP: God of the resurrection, we come to your table today having heard the words of hope spoken by Mary, "I have seen the Lord."

Mary had seen the stone rolled away from the tomb's entrance; she had seen the empty tomb and the empty grave cloths. She had experienced the emptiness of the crucifixion, the loss of all hope, and now the loss of being able to bury her Lord. She must have felt empty.

The cup on this table sits before us. It is not empty. It is filled with the great love of God. It is filled with the sacrifice of Jesus Christ. It is filled with the resurrection! We too see the Lord, experience Christ's presence, and are filled anew with hope as we drink from this cup. Amen.

UNIFIED PRAYER: We come to your table today, risen God, not in memory of that first Easter, but rather in celebration and amazement...for Jesus did not just die on the cross, but through the resurrection, became the risen Christ! We are celebrating an event that has the power to transform each of us.

Earlier this week, we ate bread and drank from the cup with dread of what was to happen that evening. Today, we again will eat bread and drink from the cup. On this day of resurrection, we eat and drink in the presence of the risen Christ, who gives hope and light to overcome all odds.

Holy Spirit, hear our prayers of thanksgiving and joy. Let us experience the risen Christ so that we, like Mary, will say, "I have seen the Lord." Amen.

STATEMENT AFTER COMMUNION: Let us remember about Easter: "As the resurrection reversed the crucifixion, so the presence of the risen Christ is found in places where reversal is taking place in today's world: in moments of salvation where the mighty are thrown down and the lowly are lifted up. As eucharist, this meal doesn't point to something way back then, nor does it point to itself inside this sanctuary. It points to the presence of Jesus Christ being revealed *out there, right now.*"*

*O. Wesley Allen, Jr., *Preaching Resurrection* (St. Louis: Chalice Press, 2000), p. 90.

Second Sunday of Easter

Acts 2:14a, 22–32
Psalm 16
1 Peter 1:3–9
John 20:19–31

PRAYER FOR THE BREAD: Creative God, you have created us with all sorts of bodies—short, tall, male, female, of many colors and shapes—and you have blessed us, saying we are created in your image. To prove it, you came in Jesus Christ, taking on flesh, like us. At the Lord's table, Jesus said, "This is my body," as he broke bread. He gave it to the disciples that they, and we, might have physical, tangible reminders that Christ is truly with us. Like Thomas, we sometimes ask for proof of your life, proof of your power. Here we see the bread that for us symbolizes the body of Christ; here we believe; here we are blessed by your presence. Through your Spirit, give us the gift of discernment, so that we may respond to the living Christ as Thomas did, saying, "My Lord and my God." Amen.

PRAYER FOR THE CUP: Life-giving God, you are our chosen portion; you are the cup of life. In this Easter season, we lift the cup of communion, celebrating the gift of life that we have received in Jesus Christ. Here, as we drink this cup, we experience the fullness of joy, recognizing that this cup of sacrifice became a cup of victory at Christ's resurrection. Here we celebrate a new birth into the living hope, because we are a resurrection people. Fill us with the joy of your Spirit. Amen.

Unified Prayer: How awesome is this place, for here we encounter your presence, holy and loving God. Here we recall the miracle of love that took place around a table in Jerusalem so many years ago. Your love was so profoundly expressed in that upper room, where you gathered with your disciples to give them a new covenant. Your love was so profoundly tested on the cross, where our Savior suffered. Your love was so profoundly vindicated at the open tomb and in the joyous announcement that Christ is risen. We thank you for the bread, for it helps us remember that your love took human form and offered itself to be broken for our sake. We thank you for the cup, for it is the cup of sacrifice and the cup of victory. Through your Spirit, let our hearts soar in joy and in love. Amen.

Prayer after Communion: We go our way with glad hearts and joyous souls, for we have been to the table of Jesus Christ, our risen Lord. Bless this moment for us, O God of joyous surprises, and help us see the presence of the risen Christ not only at this table but also throughout our lives in the days ahead. Amen.

Third Sunday of Easter

Acts 2:14a, 36–41
Psalm 116:1–4, 12–19
1 Peter 1:17–23
Luke 24:13–35

PRAYER FOR THE BREAD: You are the God of the prophets, the God of new understanding. Help us understand your word so that we may truly rejoice in this Easter season. Like the followers on the road to Emmaus, may we recognize the living Christ in the breaking of bread. Like the early believers after Pentecost, may we be known to others in the breaking of bread. Through your Spirit, work within our hearts and minds to transform our lives from fear to joy. Amen.

PRAYER FOR THE CUP: God of the risen Christ, we can scarcely begin to fathom the depths and power of your love. As we come to this moment in the communion service, we remember the words of the psalmist: "I will lift up the cup of salvation and call on the name of the LORD."* This is truly the cup of salvation, not for any magical powers of its own, but because it reminds us of the precious blood of Christ. Bless us by your Spirit as we drink from the cup today, that we may acknowledge that we are truly part of your family. Amen.

*Psalm 116:13.

UNIFIED PRAYER: God of steadfast love, sometimes we get so caught up in our own fears and anxieties that we are unaware of your presence. Walk with us on the dark roads of life, helping us understand your will and your way for us. Make our hearts burn within us as we realize the power of your life-giving love. Help us overcome our timidity, that we will beg you to come to the table with us. Help us realize your presence in the breaking of bread at this and every meal. Bless this loaf and this cup, so that as we partake, we may be truly blessed. We pray not for the transformation of the elements, but for the transformation of our lives, that we might be your Easter people. Through your Spirit, open our eyes to the awesome reality of your love. Amen.

PRAYER AFTER COMMUNION: We give you thanks, O God, for you are faithful, and your steadfast love endures forever. We give you thanks for the invitation to come to this table, a physical, symbolic expression of a love that never dies. As we leave this place, may the love and unity that we feel here travel with us in our daily lives, that others may come to know you for having seen your presence in our lives. Amen.

Fourth Sunday of Easter

Acts 2:42–47
Psalm 23
1 Peter 2:19–25
John 10:1–10

PRAYER FOR THE BREAD: With glad and generous hearts, we come to the table praising the One who made this meal possible, our Lord Jesus Christ. As together we break the bread this day, let us, like the early Christians, praise you, God. We know that in this community of believers and around this table, we celebrate not only the risen Christ, but also your reign to be on earth. Amen.

PRAYER FOR THE CUP: Shepherd God, you tenderly care for us and protect us. You have come to us through Jesus Christ, the Good Shepherd, through whom we know your voice. When we are thirsty and tired, you lead us beside the still waters, so that we might find refreshment. Here at this table, we also find that you give us refreshment and blessing when we are thirsty. Here we drink of the cup that reminds us that the Good Shepherd poured out his life to protect his flock. Bless us as we drink from this cup, that we may know the goodness of your Spirit. Amen.

UNIFIED PRAYER: O Guardian of our souls, through Jesus Christ we have come to know you as the Good Shepherd. You are a God who cares for our basic needs, a shepherd who feeds the flock with gentleness and tenderness. You know our names. You have prepared the table for us with bread and wine to nourish our souls. In this time together, gathered as Christians, we eat and drink from that which you have prepared.

We become more aware that by the wounds of our Savior Jesus Christ, *we* have been healed. We had gone astray, and he rescued us. Thank you for this wonderful gift of life. Help us, by the presence of your Spirit, to live faithfully and fully in your love. Amen.

PRAYER AFTER COMMUNION:
May you go forth strengthened and refreshed
by the table, which the Lord prepares.
May the Spirit of the Risen Christ restore your soul,
and may your lives move ever on right paths.
May you know God's presence in every valley,
and may the grace of our Lord Jesus Christ,
the love of God,
and the communion of the Holy Spirit,
be with us all. Amen.[*]

[*]Kadi Billman, in McKiernan-Allen, ed., *Celebrating Incarnation,* p. 41.

Fifth Sunday of Easter

Acts 7:55–60
Psalm 31:1–5, 15–16
1 Peter 2:2–10
John 14:1–14

PRAYER FOR THE BREAD: O God, our rock and fortress, in whom we find refuge, we offer praise that you care for us. We know we can seek help and protection from you in times of trouble.

Your presence and care is truly here at the table where we celebrate your great power of life over death. Through Jesus Christ, we see you and know your wondrous love. Through this ordinary bread, we see beyond earthly meaning. Through the eating of the bread, we see what you want us to be. Amen.

PRAYER FOR THE CUP: God of prophets and martyrs, God of everyday people, we praise you for your steadfast love. We praise you for having sent Jesus Christ, for through him we can see you and know you. We come to this table to bless this cup and to drink from it, knowing that in doing so, we experience the living Christ in our midst. Bless us as we drink from it, and give us the strength of your Spirit so that we may do the works of Christ and bring you glory. Amen.

UNIFIED PRAYER: We celebrate the risen Christ by coming to this table today. We anticipate with joy being in the presence of God's Son—the living Christ! We come to claim our heritage as God's people, chosen and filled with mercy.

The bread of heaven, the cup of hope are ours. We have tasted that the Lord is good. Teach us, God, as we go from the table nourished by this spiritual food, that we must act mercifully toward others. Teach us, God, as we go from the table, knowing that we are your chosen people, that *all* are your chosen people.

Teach us, God, as we go from the table, that we are called out of darkness to proclaim your light and your message. Amen.

PRAYER AFTER COMMUNION: God, we recognize with humility and gratitude that we are your construction project. At this table and in our daily lives, you can mold us into being a holy priesthood, a spiritual house with Jesus Christ as our cornerstone. As we leave this place, may we take the holiness with us, so that it slowly transforms us, step-by-step, into the image of Jesus Christ. Amen.

Sixth Sunday of Easter

Acts 17:22–31
Psalm 66:8–20
1 Peter 3:13–22
John 14:15–21

PRAYER FOR THE BREAD:
"Lord of our highest love! Let now your peace be
given;
fix all our thoughts on things above, our hearts on you
in heaven.
Then dearest Christ, draw near, while we your table
spread;
and crown the feast with heavenly cheer, yourself the
living bread.
And when the loaf we break, your own rich blessing
give,
may all with loving hearts partake and all new
strength receive."* Amen.

PRAYER FOR THE CUP: Steadfast God, we praise you for
listening to our prayers and keeping us in your great
love. We never feel abandoned, because of your
presence. In times of great trial, we are assured that you
are always with us.

The cup on this table is given to us out of the greatest
of trials. Jesus Christ, our Savior, had to die for us to
receive this cup. But out of this trial came a triumph—
life over death! Evil is overcome; Christ lives.

*G. Y. Tickle, "Lord of Our Highest Love" (19th century).

As we drink from this cup of life, may it give us strength to persevere through difficult times so that we can witness to God's will. Amen.

UNIFIED PRAYER: O God of promise fulfilled, we thank you for the gift of the Holy Spirit to dwell within us. Because of the Spirit's presence, we know we will never be alone. Because our Savior lives, we will live also; we are assured of that.

That is why we come to the table today—to celebrate life! The Easter message is timeless and forever. Jesus lives! This is the bread of life and the cup of sacrifice. They are ours as a gift of grace.

Holy Spirit, we welcome your presence in our midst as we celebrate the Easter message of resurrection. Amen.

PRAYER AFTER COMMUNION:
"O Jesus, strong in gentleness,
come now yourself our hearts possess,
that we may give you all our days
the tribute of our grateful praise.
Come, risen Christ, with us abide
in this our joyful Eastertide;
your own redeemed forever shield
from ev'ry weapon death can wield."* Amen.

---

*"That Easter Day with Joy Was Bright," Latin hymn (5th century), trans. John Mason Neale, 1852.

Seventh Sunday of Easter

Acts 1:6–14
Psalm 68:1–10, 32–35
1 Peter 4:12–14; 5:6–11
John 17:1–11

PRAYER FOR THE BREAD: We come to this table in song, dear God, praising your name and seeking your guidance. In a busy and mundane world, we often fail to see your glory, to acknowledge your power. Here, we come and reenact the mystery of the Christ, who gave of himself for us, who offered his life that we might live. In eating this bread, we affirm this mystery and seek your blessing. Through your Spirit, give us insight and wisdom that we might accept the love you have offered us here. Amen.

PRAYER FOR THE CUP: Often, patient God, we go through the motions of faith and belief and don't take it seriously. Break through our indifference and apathy, so that we may realize that this quiet place is filled with your glory. Help us be aware that we are truly in the presence of the living God. May the cup that we now offer for your blessing help us to know that your blessings are poured out on us in so many ways. Through your Spirit, transform us so that we may truly be your disciples. Amen.

UNIFIED PRAYER: How awesome you are, O God. You are beyond human comprehension, and yet we can experience your presence in our lives. Through the resurrection of Christ and the gift of your Spirit, you show us your compassion and your power. Help us to learn to trust in that compassion and power. Help us, like the earliest disciples, to be so filled with your presence that we carry your good news to all who will hear. We come to this table because you have invited us, so that we may receive the gift of the risen Christ, and so that we might experience your glory. Give us humble spirits and open, receptive hearts as we eat this bread and as we drink this wine. Help us see beyond our own needs and purposes to become a part of your purpose, to be faithful disciples. May we not be so full of ourselves, so that we may become full of your Spirit. Amen.

PRAYER AFTER COMMUNION: Surprising God, when Jesus ascended to be with you in glory, you sent your angel to tell the disciples to stop staring into the empty space where Jesus had been, and to go spread the good news of Christ's victory. We have cherished these moments at your table. Now help us realize that the Christ who was with us here is the Christ who is with us out there. Redirect our vision and renew our energy, so that we might go into the world to live the good news. Amen.

Day of Pentecost

Acts 2:1–21 or *Numbers 11:24–30*
Psalm 104:24–34, 35b
1 Corinthians 12:3b–13 or *Acts 2:1–21*
John 20:19–23 or *John 7:37–39*

PRAYER FOR THE BREAD: Creative God, how you must delight in diversity. All around the world, believers of different colors and languages, nations and social classes, ages and abilities, come together at your table, and you welcome them all! Although all our differences are real, we find here the unity of your Spirit that draws us together. As bread is broken and eaten around the world, we proclaim that with all our rich diversity, we are one. We are Christ's body. We are Christ's people. Help us through your Spirit to live as though we believe it. Amen.

PRAYER FOR THE CUP: Living, loving God, bless us by your Spirit as we come to drink from this cup. Help us realize that as we are baptized in your name, we drink not only from a physical cup, but from your Spirit as well. Through your Spirit, you offer us the living water of Christ's love, the living water that gives us life. On this Pentecost Sunday, we pray that your Spirit will refresh us and restore us, so that we might live lives of joy and peace. Amen.

UNIFIED PRAYER: Breathe your Spirit upon us, O living God. Fill us with new life. Transform us into your image. Touch our hearts, that we might love as you would have us love. Open our eyes so that we may discern the gifts of the Spirit that you have given each one of us. On this Pentecost Sunday, we gather, eager, expectant, and maybe a little frightened, waiting for the Spirit that Christ has promised us. Now we come to your table, being aware of another promise of Christ, that someday we will eat bread and drink wine in glory with him. For now, though, we have your Spirit, and that is enough. Bless us as we eat, bless us as we drink, so that we may bless you in prayer, praise, and service. Amen.

PRAYER AFTER COMMUNION: God of love, we have reenacted here how Christ and the disciples gathered in the upper room to break bread and drink wine. God of Spirit, we have remembered how thousands gathered to receive your Spirit in the upper room on Pentecost. Bless us now as we go from this, our own upper room, to be witnesses in word and deed of Christ's redeeming love. Amen.

Trinity Sunday (First Sunday after Pentecost)

Genesis 1:1–2:4a
Psalm 8
2 Corinthians 13:11–13
Matthew 28:16–20

PRAYER FOR THE BREAD:
"For the beauty of the earth, for the glory of the skies,
for the love which from our birth over and around us
lies,
Lord of all, to thee we raise this our hymn of grateful
praise."*

We come to your table this day not at all comprehending how you could take nothingness and create such a wonderful world. And yet you didn't stop there. You created us, your children, to live in your world. And when we needed to be shown how to live, you sent your very own Son to show us. The bread, made from the grain of your creation, helps us remember that your Son, Jesus, gave his life for us.

"For thy church that evermore lifteth holy hands
above,
offering up on every shore one pure sacrifice of love,
Lord of all, to thee we raise this our hymn of grateful
praise."* Amen.

PRAYER FOR THE CUP: How clear, O God, were your Son's instructions to his disciples when he said, "Go into all the world and make disciples of all the nations." Help us

*Folliot S. Pierpoint, "For the Beauty of the Earth" (1864).

live out our conviction with the confession that Jesus is the Christ and follow the mandate given by your Son. Jesus gave his very life to show your great love for us. In this cup is his lifeblood—his conviction of being your Son. We drink from the cup, and we know you will be with us to the end of the age. Amen.

UNIFIED PRAYER: "It is very good to gather here at the hearth of God's creativity, where the hope of the world was kneaded into the One who said, 'This is my body, given for you.'

It is very good to drink at this table from the deep cup of hope, taking the promise from the One who said, 'This cup is the new covenant in my blood.'

Here at this table the drama of creation continues, creating an unbroken line from Maker to Redeemer to Comforter.

Here we step onto the stage and take our part in the divine liturgy, taking on Christ's brokenness and generous spilling for all of creation.

Come, taste, and see that the Lord is good."* Amen.

PRAYER AFTER COMMUNION: You are the God of far-off galaxies, yet you are the God who cares for each of your children individually. You sent us Jesus the Christ so that we might know you. You have given us this table so that we might experience Christ in our midst. We bless you as we go from this holy place, and pray that your Spirit may bless us as we go into your holy world. Amen.

---

*Laura Loving, in McKiernan-Allen, ed., *Celebrating Incarnation*, p. 9.

Proper 4*
Sunday between May 29 and June 4

Genesis 6:9–22; 7:24; 8:14–19
Psalm 46
Romans 1:16–17; 3:22b–28, (29–31)
Matthew 7:21–29

PRAYER FOR THE BREAD: O God of certainty, we come before you in times of many changes. We never know from day to day what our lives and our world may unfold to be. But we always know you are there giving us refuge and strength, that we need not know fear. As we take this loaf and eat, give us strength in your Son, our Savior, Jesus Christ, who gave his life so we may know you are indeed our God. Amen.

PRAYER FOR THE CUP:

> "On Christ the solid rock I stand,
> all other ground is sinking sand.
> His oath, his covenant, his blood
> support me in the whelming flood.
> When all around my soul gives way,
> he then is all my hope and stay.
> On Christ the solid rock I stand,
> all other ground is sinking sand."**

God, help our faith to be solidly built in you. We thank you for your Son, Jesus Christ, and his life, death, and resurrection, that we may have life in you. This cup of the new covenant gives us strength to be wise caregivers in your holy reign. Amen.

*For Propers 1–3, see pp. 32–37.
**Edward Mote, "My Hope Is Built" (1834).

UNIFIED PRAYER: God of us all, we know that something symbolic is not "just" a symbol. This Sunday as every Sunday, we gather at the table and speak of the bread—symbolic of the broken body—and the cup—symbolic of the shed blood. These symbols are more than mere tokens of worship and faith; they are, rather, deep and powerful expressions of our participation in the body and blood of Christ, of our solidarity with the suffering and sacrifice of Christ, of our partnership in the life of the resurrected Christ. With the eating and drinking of these symbols, we celebrate with all your children. Amen.

PRAYER AFTER COMMUNION: In the midst of our frantic, noisy lives, we have come to this table, O God of peace. Here we have responded to your command, "Be still and know that I am God." Let the stillness and holiness of this place center our lives in you, even as we go back into our daily lives. Amen.

Proper 5
Sunday between June 5 and 11

> Genesis 12:1–9
> Psalm 33:1–12
> Romans 4:13–25
> Matthew 9:9–13, 18–26

PRAYER FOR THE BREAD: Forgiving God, we come to this table today confessing that we have sinned against you and your people. Because you have provided this bread for us, we know that you will forgive us our sins. We realize that the bread reminds us of the body of your Son, who died for the forgiveness of all. Merciful God, we thank you for your forgiveness; help us to follow you more fully. Amen.

PRAYER FOR THE CUP: God of Abram and Sarai, we seek your presence as we continue on our own journey of faith. We hold to your promises in seeking meaning for our daily lives. We drink from this cup, which gives us strength to journey in your love. The cup, the blood of Jesus the Christ, fulfills the promise you gave Abram. Strengthen our faith as we seek to do your will. Amen.

UNIFIED PRAYER: O healing God, we call upon your name to make us whole. And being a merciful God, you heal us far beyond what we would ever dream. By our faith, we come to this meal knowing that wholeness in your name is made possible by your Son, Jesus Christ. The bread of healing and the cup of wholeness are gifts given to each of us. Holy Spirit, keep our faith strong as we seek to do your will. Amen.

PRAYER AFTER COMMUNION: God, you have called us all to journeys of faith, and you accompany us along the way. Here at this table, we have received nourishment for the journey. Thank you for these gifts. Amen.

Proper 6
Sunday between June 12 and 18

Genesis 18:1–15, (21:1–7)
Psalm 116:1–2, 12–19
Romans 5:1–8
Matthew 9:35–10:8, (9–23)

PRAYER FOR THE BREAD: Like Abraham and Sarah, we come to this table confessing that we do not always believe our prayers will be answered. Like Abraham and Sarah, we do not always believe what we hear as an answer to our prayers. And like Abraham and Sarah, we do not always recognize your presence when you are with us. Forgive us these sins and help us to have a deeper faith. Now, as we eat from this broken loaf, help us recognize the One who is the answer to all our prayers, Jesus Christ, in whom our salvation comes. Amen.

PRAYER FOR THE CUP: At this table, we lift the cup of salvation and call upon your name, O Lord. We give you thanks, for you have heard our prayers and have given us your Son, Jesus Christ, in whom our salvation comes. In drinking from this cup of sacrifice we enter into a new covenant with you, a covenant of your love for us in Jesus Christ and our love and commitment to you. Amen.

UNIFIED PRAYER: Giver of hope that does not disappoint, we approach your table because your love has been poured into our hearts by the Holy Spirit. We eat the bread and drink from the cup that are before us, knowing that we are undeserving. Yet as you have given us your grace, the bread and cup are also given to each of us through our Lord Jesus Christ because of your great love. We thank you for your hope, love, grace, and most of all for your Son. Amen.

PRAYER AFTER COMMUNION: God, help us to bring your reign here on earth. Give us strength to proclaim your words of salvation and healing, of joy and hope, of answered prayer. We seek the presence of your Spirit to be with us in our ministries. Amen.

Proper 7
Sunday between June 19 and 25

Genesis 21:8–21
Psalm 86:1–10, 16–17
Romans 6:1b–11
Matthew 10:24–39

PRAYER FOR THE BREAD: O listening God, we know you hear us when we call out to you. In our need we seek you. As you answered Hagar and helped her, we know you will answer and help us. We seek a Savior; we seek renewed life without sin. And here before us is the symbol of the very One we seek. The bread is our Savior's body, given for us. The nourishment it gives us is an answer to our prayers. Amen.

PRAYER FOR THE CUP: The path of following your Son, God, is difficult. We have to make choices, be committed, set priorities, and be intentional. In our busy, frantic, and fragmented lives, this isn't always easy. We know that you will give us guidance and strength to live the life worthy of Christ.

You have made these choices on our behalf. We are assured of our value and worth. Jesus has told us that not even a sparrow falls to the ground but that the Father knows.

We are reassured that you made the commitment for all your children when you sent your Son, Jesus Christ. This cup on the table is witness to your commitment; it is life overcoming death.

Holy Spirit, guide our paths into commitment to Christ. Amen.

UNIFIED PRAYER: God of new life, we praise you this day for all that you have done for us. We especially thank you for your Son, Jesus Christ, and the new life he gives to all who follow him.

The bread and cup on the table are a sign of resurrection, of triumph of life over death. You transformed Jesus' death into life with you. And then you offered this life eternal to each of us. We have died in Christ to live with him.

The sharing of this meal signifies a new way of life for each of us—a life without sin. Holy Spirit, guide our lives that they will be made new in Christ. Amen.

PRAYER AFTER COMMUNION:
> "We thank thee that thy Church, unsleeping
> while earth rolls onward into light,
> through all the world her watch is keeping,
> and rests not now by day or night."[*]

Let us go into the world, strengthened by the bread and cup, witnessing to the reign of God. Amen.

[*]John Ellerton, "The Day Thou Gavest, Lord, Is Ended" (1870).

Proper 8
Sunday between June 26 and July 2

> *Genesis 22:1–14*
> *Psalm 13*
> *Romans 6:12–23*
> *Matthew 10:40–42*

PRAYER FOR THE BREAD: O steadfast God, it is easy for us to believe that you have forsaken us when we are in sorrow and despair. Forgive us when we think you are absent. We realize you are always present with us in the Holy Spirit. Help us to trust in your love, rejoice in your salvation, and sing praises to you.

We praise you most in the eating of this bread, the body of our Lord and Savior. And we know you are always with us as we receive spiritual nourishment from this meal. Amen.

PRAYER FOR THE CUP: Increase our faith and trust in you, God of Abraham. Help us to know that you will always provide for us in whatever situation we may find ourselves. Help us move out of our sinful lives into a grace-filled life that will reflect your encompassing love. We are at this table today to drink from the cup of eternal life given to us by your Son, Jesus Christ. Holy Spirit, come, be with us as we drink from the cup, our thirst quenched. Amen.

UNIFIED PRAYER: At this table, all are welcome: the saint and the sinner, the poor and the rich, the men and the women, the married and single. At this table all may eat: the privileged and the marginalized, the gay and the straight, the powerful and the powerless. At this table, all may drink: the young and the old, the infirm and the well, the slaves and the free.

For God's mercy is wide, God's blessing is kind, and God's reward is great. The cup of cold water, the cup of the new covenant, and the bread of life are ours to take and ours to share in your name, Savior of the world. Amen.

PRAYER AFTER COMMUNION: Give us, O God, the courage to live a life of faith and trust, of welcoming and receiving, of grace and holiness. Let us go from this table renewed, to do your will on Earth. Amen.

Proper 9
Sunday between July 3 and 9

Genesis 24:34–38, 42–49, 58–67
Psalm 45:10–17
Romans 7:15–25a
Matthew 11:16–19, 25–30

PRAYER FOR THE BREAD: O steadfast God, it is hard to be Christian in our world. We try to please our friends and coworkers, our families and our supervisors. We try to be agreeable to those whom we meet while shopping and friendly to those who help us. Yet we receive mixed messages from them. We seem to not know what is expected of us in this world.

We are so thankful, God, that your law is constant. We know that to please you, we will obey you. It is more important for us to obey and please you than to worry about those around us.

We obey your law of love in the eating of this bread, the body of Jesus who gave his life for us. Holy Spirit, strengthen us by this holy meal to always obey our God. Amen.

PRAYER FOR THE CUP:
"I bind my heart this tide to the Galilean's side,
to the wounds of Calvary, to the Christ who died for me.
I bind my soul this day to the brother far away,
and the sister near at hand, in this town, and in this land.
I bind my heart in thrall to the God, the Lord of all,

to the God, the poor ones' friend, and the Christ
whom God did send.
I bind myself to peace, to make strife and envy cease,
God, knit thou sure the cord of my thraldom to my
Lord."*

At the table of the Christ who died for all of us, we come to celebrate a sacred, yet common cup. We come to celebrate a commitment to a new way of life. We come to drink from the cup of the new covenant poured out for us. O Christ, we commit ourselves to follow you. Amen.

UNIFIED PRAYER: Sometimes, God, you surprise us and ask us to do something that we have never considered. As with Abraham's servant whom you asked to fetch a wife for Isaac; as with Rebekah, who happened to be at the well; as with Paul, who happened to be on a road leading to Damascus, you enter our lives and ask us to do a task for you.

There are times when we do not want to do this; we want to do what we have always done and be comfortable with things the way they are. Forgive us when we do not listen to you. Help us to take your yoke and learn from you. Help us to answer yes to your call.

Our hunger is assuaged, our thirst is quenched at this table. We find our way to Jesus here. We find rest for our souls in you. We go empowered by the Holy Spirit, to answer to your surprises. Amen.

STATEMENT AFTER COMMUNION: Thanks be to God through Jesus Christ our Lord for this meal that we have shared!

* Lauchlan MacLean Watt, "I Bind My Heart This Tide" (1907).

Proper 10
Sunday between July 10 and 16

Genesis 25:19–34
Psalm 119:105–112
Romans 8:1–11
Matthew 13:1–9, 18–23

PRAYER FOR THE BREAD:

"Spirit of God, descend upon my heart;
wean it from earth, through all its pulses move;
stoop to my weakness, mighty as thou art,
and make me love thee as I ought to love."[*]

O God, you have given us Jesus Christ, your Son, to die for us. You have given us the Holy Spirit to be with us always. You have given us not only life but life eternal. In the eating of this bread reminding us of the body of Jesus, let us dwell in the Spirit and in peace. Amen.

PRAYER FOR THE CUP:

"Cup of sorrow, cup of joy,
filling souls that come in thirst,
likewise, we shall fill the cups
of those who thirst throughout the earth."[**]

O God who quenches the thirst of all who seek you, help us to spread the word of your kingdom to those who thirst, that the word might be understood, bearing fruit, yielding and increasing those who love and glorify you. Amen.

[*]George Croly, "Spirit of God, Descend upon My Heart" (1867).
[**]Peter Olejar, "Now We Come Before God's Presence" (1992), © 1995 Chalice Press.

84

UNIFIED PRAYER: O God, your Holy Word is a lamp to our feet and a light to our paths; lead us in doing your will on earth. We confess that our paths are not always your ways; we are too influenced by the ways that look easy and profitable for us. Forgive us when we take the wrong path in our lives.

At this table where we eat the bread of heaven and drink from the cup of life, nourish our souls and refresh our lives. Let us look to Jesus and follow his examples as we live the Christian life. Amen.

STATEMENT AFTER COMMUNION: Send us forth as people who hear with their ears, see with their eyes, and understand with their hearts, that your word might bear fruit within us and through us.[*]

---

[*]Phyllis Cole and Everett Tilson, *Litanies and Other Prayers for Year A* (Nashville: Abingdon Press, 1992), p. 111.

Proper 11
Sunday between July 17 and 23

Genesis 28:10–19a
Psalm 139:1–12, 23–24
Romans 8:12–25
Matthew 13:24–30, 36–43

PRAYER FOR THE BREAD:
"All the world is God's own field,
fruit unto His praise to yield;
Wheat and tares together sown,
unto joy or sorrow grown;
First the blade, and then the ear,
then the full corn shall appear.
Lord of harvest, grant that we
wholesome grain and pure may be.
Even so, Lord, quickly come
to thy final harvest home;
Gather Thou Thy people in,
free from sorrow, free from sin,
There, forever purified,
in Thy garner to abide:
Come, with all Thine angels, come,
raise the glorious harvest home."*
The fruits of the harvest are here in the loaf. Come, the
commitment we offer in the eating of the bread. Amen.

*Henry Alford, "Come, Ye Thankful People, Come" (1844).

PRAYER FOR THE CUP: Ever-present God, we feel your presence everyday in our lives. We wish to experience it to the fullest; mold us by the Holy Spirit to lead lives worthy of Christ Jesus. In the cross of Jesus Christ is your love and mercy for us. You have chosen us as your heirs, your children.

At this holy table and in the drinking from this cup, we sense your love, mercy, and presence. Through Christ's death and resurrection we see your intent for your children—life in you. The cup, Christ's commitment to following your will, is ours.

Holy Spirit, sent by God and in Christ Jesus, lead and guide us into lives worthy of being heirs. Amen.

UNIFIED PRAYER: Surely the Lord is in this place where we worship this day! Like Jacob, we feel your presence, God, when our rest is hard. Like David, we feel your presence in the bad times of our lives as well as the good times. You have known us from our very conception, and we are assured you will be with us all of our lives.

This table is a table of hope; we are believing in Jesus Christ's resurrection, though we have not seen. We are believing because we feel God's presence in our lives. God, you have given us this bread and cup just as you have given us your Son, Jesus Christ. We eat and drink at the table in the presence of your gift of the Holy Spirit. Amen.

STATEMENT AFTER COMMUNION: Thanks be to God! We have felt God's presence in all places and spaces in creation. We have especially felt God's presence in this holy meal today. Thanks be to God!

Proper 12
Sunday between July 24 and 30

Genesis 29:15–28
Psalm 105:1–11, 45b or *Psalm 128*
Romans 8:26–39
Matthew 13:31–33, 44–52

PRAYER FOR THE BREAD: O God, you take ordinary people such as Jacob, Leah, and Rachel and make a nation. You take ordinary, everyday things such as a mustard seed, yeast, a field, or fishing nets and help us understand about your reign. You take ordinary bread and an extraordinary love and show us your Son, our Savior.

Let our ordinary lives be nourished by the eating of the bread as we seek, by the power of the Holy Spirit, to do your work. Amen.

PRAYER FOR THE CUP: It is hard to think of your reign, O Holy God. We are so immersed in our own world and its commitments; it is easy for us to think that those values are the most important in our lives. Then we hear the words of Jesus. Your kingdom is worth more than we will ever have in material things. Your kingdom is like a fine pearl causing us to rid ourselves of everything we own just to have it.

Forgive us, God, when we have our priorities wrong about what is of value to us. Help us, like the yeast a woman adds to the flour, be spiritual leaven in your world. We receive your forgiveness as we take the cup this day, remembering that Christ made our forgiveness possible by his death and resurrection. Thank you for this greatest of treasures. Amen.

UNIFIED PRAYER: From a world filled with war, poverty, racism, personal tragedy, and stress we come into your sanctuary. Here we hope to find peace, justice, equality, and tranquility. We know that when we are too deep in despair to utter words to you, you send your Spirit to pray for us. Help us to internalize that all things work together for good for those who love you. Help us to have confidence that nothing in this world can separate us from your love.

At this table with the bread and cup set before us, we feel the presence of the Holy Spirit. Let the nourishment we receive from this bread and wine empower us to move into a deeper faith with you. O ever-present God, we praise you. Amen.

PRAYER AFTER COMMUNION: Thank you, gracious God, for this time together at your holy table. May this time sustain us in all our times, good and bad, in the week ahead. And may we seek out ways to live out the love that you have given us. Amen.

Proper 13
Sunday between July 31 and August 6

Genesis 32:22–31
Psalm 17:1–7, 15
Romans 9:1–5
Matthew 14:13–21

PRAYER FOR THE BREAD:
Through all gifts of creation,
your children have been fed.
Through manna in the wilderness,
your children have been fed.
Through loaves and fishes distributed on a hillside,
your children have been fed.
Through your living word, sustaining our spirits and
guiding the church,
your children have been fed.
Through pastors and teachers who have taught us
your way,
your children have been fed.
Through the living bread that we receive at this table,
and through the living Christ in our midst,
your children are now being fed.
Gracious God, living Christ, loving Spirit, we thank
you. Amen.

PRAYER FOR THE CUP: God, you are the Good Shepherd,
and you lead your people as a flock. We thank you for
sending us Jesus Christ to be our Shepherd, and for his
willingness to give of his life so that we may live. As we
drink from this cup, we remember Christ's life and Christ's
love poured out for us, and affirm his living presence

with us. Bless us as we drink, that we may know your Spirit's tender care in our lives. Amen.

UNIFIED PRAYER: When your children are lost and alone, you guide us. When your children are hungry, you feed us. When your children thirst, you refresh us. Thank you, loving God, for sustaining us when we are in need. The feast that we now celebrate is a symbol of your grace and kindness. Thank you for the gifts of bread and wine, and thank you that through them we are aware of the greatest gift, our Savior Jesus Christ. Touch our lives with holiness, so that our lives may reflect your love. Amen.

PRAYER AFTER COMMUNION: Here, gracious God, we have found refreshment and rest. Here we have been fed and watered by your hand. May your Spirit continue to guide us, and may we follow as your faithful flock. Amen.

Proper 14
Sunday between August 7 and 13

Genesis 37:1–4, 12–28
Psalm 105:1–6, 16–22, 45b
Romans 10:5–15
Matthew 14:22–33

PRAYER FOR THE BREAD: Faithful God, we come to worship you, knowing that through Jesus Christ you can still the storms of our lives with the words "Peace, be still." In the midst of a violent culture and world of stress and conflict, Christ touches our lives and transforms them. Help us, like the disciples of old, to be able to say, "Truly, you are the Son of God." The bread that we break and eat in this service of communion is symbolic of Christ's love for us. We pray that through your Spirit, it will also be symbolic of our love for Christ. Amen.

PRAYER FOR THE CUP: God of grace, we know that you love all your children and that in you all the walls of human separation and conflict will crumble. As we gather at this table to drink from this cup, we remember that Christ's last meal with the disciples was set in the midst of conflict and hatred; yet seeds were planted there that grew and blossomed in the triumph of love, the resurrection of Christ. Let us, through your Spirit, find here the seeds of peace and hope that will help us witness your love to everybody. Amen.

UNIFIED PRAYER: We give you thanks, wonderful God, and sing your praises. In you, we find strength and support in all of life's troubles. We gather here to remember that even when Jesus faced his own death on the cross, he gathered his disciples together in the upper room to feed them and bring them strength. Thus, when we gather here, we too find nurture and strength in your steadfast love. The elements that we share here point beyond themselves and help us recall that Christ gave up everything so that we might have life. Bless us with your Spirit as we eat and drink, so that your love may draw us together. Amen.

PRAYER AFTER COMMUNION: Here at this table you have set before us, O God, we have affirmed that the Christ who died is the Christ who lives. As we leave, we pray that we may be aware of the risen Christ who walks with us each step of the way. Amen.

Proper 15
Sunday between August 14 and 20

> Genesis 45:1–15
> Psalm 133
> Romans 11:1–2a, 29–32
> Matthew 15:(10–20), 21–28

PRAYER FOR THE BREAD: Gracious God, you have not limited your love to those of one group or nationality, nor to those who are worthy. Rather, your grace and love extend to all who call on your name. Give us a humble spirit as we gather here, so that we may realize we are not worthy; but also give us a spirit of courage and faith, so that we will not be afraid to ask for what we need. As we break bread together, let us receive it joyfully as a gift freely given, just as Jesus Christ freely gave of himself for our healing and salvation. Bind us together in your Spirit with all your children, and make us a community of healing and grace. Amen.

PRAYER FOR THE CUP: Faithful God, you enter into covenants with your children, and you never forsake nor abandon them. We thank you for all the covenants you have made that have kept your word alive through the centuries. We especially thank you for the covenant that Jesus Christ made with the disciples in the upper room. For when he took the cup, he gave thanks for it and said, "Drink from it, all of you; for this is my blood of the covenant, which is poured out for many for the forgiveness of sins."* This is the covenant that we renew

*Matthew 26:27b–28.

today, the covenant in which we find forgiveness, healing, and new life. Blessed is your Spirit, which is the source of our unity. Amen.

UNIFIED PRAYER: How very good and pleasant it is when we can gather together in unity around your table, O God of peace. Here we can lay aside our differences of politics, personality, class, and race, and celebrate the fact that in Christ Jesus we are one. We break bread, share it, and eat together as sisters and brothers in Christ. We bless the cup, pour it, and drink as one family gathered in love. Thank you for this precious gift of unity that brings us to your family table. Keep us united through your Spirit, so that all who see us may know that we are children of a loving God. Amen.

PRAYER AFTER COMMUNION: We have been together at your table, amazing and awesome God. It is a table of memory and hope, a table of unity and love. Here we have experienced the presence of the living Christ in our midst. Thank you. Thank you. Amen.

Proper 16
Sunday between August 21 and 27

Exodus 1:8–2:10
Psalm 124
Romans 12:1–8
Matthew 16:13–20

PRAYER FOR THE BREAD: You have prepared a table for us, Holy God, not because we are worthy, but because we are needy; not because we are good, but because we are hungry. Here, as we eat this bread, we acknowledge that Jesus Christ is our living bread, our perfect sacrifice, through whom we are fed and filled, and by whom we are redeemed. Sanctify us through your Spirit, that we may be living sacrifices, helping make the world a sacred place, filled with your love. Amen.

PRAYER FOR THE CUP: In this troubled world, liberating God, it is easy to fall into the slavery of fears and prejudice, class and ideology, possessions and payments. Yet you offer us freedom. You heard the cries of the Israelites, and through Moses have freed them from slavery. You heard the cries of all your children, and through Jesus Christ have freed them from sin. As we drink this cup, we remember the new covenant that Jesus Christ offered in the upper room. Give us the grace and courage to accept that covenant, the covenant of love, so that we might experience and share with others the freedom you would have us know. May your Spirit work within our hearts and in this congregation, that we might be your people, freed and forgiven. Amen.

UNIFIED PRAYER: When we think of how your story unfolds in the pages of the Bible and the life of the church, leader God, we are amazed. Through the centuries, through the millennia, you have called your children to follow the Way of life. When your children have turned away, you have tenderly called them home. Here at this table, we catch a glimpse of that home, we have a hint of the banquet that you prepare for your people. Here, as we eat this bread and drink this wine, we celebrate the love you have given us in Jesus Christ. May your Spirit bless us in this holy time, so that the love of Christ may transform our lives, so that others may see your love through us. Amen.

PRAYER AFTER COMMUNION: At this table, gracious God, we have received the banquet of Christ's love. At this table, God of life, we have affirmed the new life we have received in Jesus Christ. At this table, calling God, we have proclaimed that Jesus Christ is your Son and the world's Savior. Bless us as we go from this place, that we might live faithfully for you. Amen.

Proper 17
Sunday between August 28 and September 3

Exodus 3:1–15
Psalm 105:1–6, 23–26, 45c
Romans 12:9–21
Matthew 16:21–28

PRAYER FOR THE BREAD: O God of the burning bush and God who speaks to Moses and to us, we stand on holy ground at your table. You are the God of Abraham, of Isaac, of Jacob, and of Moses. You are the God and Father of Jesus Christ. And we praise you, for you are our God. As in your presence the ground before Moses was made holy, in your presence this ordinary bread is made holy.

You gave your Son to be our Savior. This holy bread helps us remember that Jesus gave his life for our sake. May the eating of the bread nourish us to do your work in our world. Amen.

PRAYER FOR THE CUP: By accepting this cup and remembering it is the blood of our Savior, your Son, we also accept the way of Christian life as Paul directed us: Love one another, hate what is evil, hold fast to what is good, be enthusiastic, serve the Lord, rejoice in hope, be patient in suffering, persevere in prayer, be generous and hospitable, and live in harmony with all. In living the Christian life, we serve all your people, God, and we serve, praise, and remember you and make your deeds known among your people. Amen.

UNIFIED PRAYER: Here is an open invitation to all who will come to remember Christ! It is our opportunity to encounter the Holy! "Yet at this table, we are beloved guests. Christ has invited all who are followers of the Way to share in the feast. Here we find 'a land flowing with milk and honey,' for in a simple cup and loaf, there is sustenance and sweetness for our souls."* Amen.

PRAYER AFTER COMMUNION: You are the God of the burning bush, a holy and awesome God. You are the God of the broken loaf, a gentle, loving God. We thank you for these moments of communion, and ask your continued presence with us as we go from this place. Amen.

*Christy Bristow, in McKiernan-Allen, ed., *Celebrating Incarnation,* p. 22.

Proper 18
Sunday between September 4 and 10

> Exodus 12:1–14
> Psalm 149
> Romans 13:8–14
> Matthew 18:15–20

PRAYER FOR THE BREAD: We praise you, wonderful God. We sing a new song before you. We bless your holy name. We are glad, for you are our creator and defender. You have redeemed us through Jesus Christ, and you have given us Christ's Spirit. This bread we offer to you, mixed and baked by human hands from the grain you created. Consecrate it, so that in sharing and eating, Christ's presence may be made real to us. Consecrate us through your Spirit, so that we may be your holy people, a blessing to our community and to the world around us. Amen.

PRAYER FOR THE CUP: You have called us to be a distinctive people, Redeemer God, with values that shine like a light on a mountaintop. Here at this table, we affirm that what sets us apart is love. We are marked by the love that you give us and by the love that we give to others. The cup we now drink reminds us that your love for us is so great that Christ's blood was shed for us. Bless us by your Spirit, so that we may walk faithfully the paths of love, bringing reconciliation and peace. Amen.

UNIFIED PRAYER: You are the God of Passover, the God of the upper room. You are the God who wants freedom for your children, the God who has called us to live in a community of love. We gather around this table to remember and to celebrate your mighty acts throughout history, especially your act of sending Jesus Christ to live and love among us, to show us your way. Consecrate this bread that we break, and this cup that we lift up, so that in sharing this meal we may realize your presence. Give us the gift of memory, to recall the sacrifice that Jesus made for us. Give us the gift of presence, so that we may be intensely aware of the living Christ in our midst. Give us the gift of hope, so that we may know that one day you will take us unto yourself. Through your Spirit, may we live in freedom and love always. Amen.

PRAYER AFTER COMMUNION: Jesus Christ has given us the promise: "For where two or three are gathered in my name, I am there among them."* Let us go from this table assured that this promise can be trusted, assured that the living Christ was here with us, assured that whenever we gather to do acts of worship, mercy, and love, the living Christ will be there. Amen.

*Matthew 18:20.

Proper 19
Sunday between September 11 and 17

Exodus 14:19–31
Psalm 114 or Exodus 15:1b–11, 20–21
Romans 14:1–12
Matthew 18:21–35

PRAYER FOR THE BREAD: Before we break bread, forgiving God, help us forgive those who have hurt us. Help us to receive forgiveness from those we have wronged. Teach us to forgive ourselves and to receive your forgiveness. Give us the realization that it is not stern and judgmental spirits you want, but loving and compassionate ones. Then, when we break the bread, our hearts will be open and receptive, our spirits humble and compassionate. Transform us through your Spirit that we may be more Christlike, so that your love may reach through us to others. Amen.

PRAYER FOR THE CUP: Life-giving God, you can turn the rocks of the desert into pools of living water, stones of dry flint into springs of water. We are a thirsty people, with a thirst that no beverage on Earth can satisfy—we thirst for meaning, for purpose, for dignity, for forgiveness, for love. Here, as we come to your table, we drink from a small cup, and yet we are refreshed and satisfied. Here,we drink from the cup that recalls the new covenant, the covenant of forgiveness. As your forgiveness is poured out on us through Jesus Christ, teach us by your Spirit to be a gentle and forgiving people. Amen.

UNIFIED PRAYER: God of power and might, you are our strength and salvation. Although there is still terrible evil in the world, we affirm that the victory is ultimately yours. As we gather at this communion table, we affirm that a single teacher and his disciples gathered in an upper room had more power than a thousand armies. Here at this table, recalling that Thursday evening of long ago, we affirm that the living Christ is with us now, giving us life and hope. We eat bread and remember that you took on human flesh in Jesus Christ, standing up to the powers of death and oppression. We drink wine and remember that Christ's sacrifice offers us the promise of forgiveness and redemption. Keep us strong in your Spirit, that we may be your faithful, forgiving people. Amen.

PRAYER AFTER COMMUNION: Leading, saving God, you guide your children from slavery to freedom. Here at this table, we have learned the secret of spiritual freedom; we have received the friendship of our Lord Jesus Christ. As we face difficult and confusing situations in the days ahead, may this friendship with Christ, which we have felt here, give us guidance and courage. Amen.

Proper 20
Sunday between September 18 and 24

Exodus 16:2–15
Psalm 105:1–6, 37–45
Philippians 1:21–30
Matthew 20:1–16

PRAYER FOR THE BREAD: Through the ages, Redeemer God, you have come to set your people free. We remember your mighty acts when they were hungry in the wilderness and you sent them holy manna. In gathering at this table, we remember another mighty act, when Jesus Christ offered his life for ours. As we break bread in Christ's name, help us remember with gratitude and adoration Christ's mighty act of setting us free. Through your Spirit, guide us so that our freedom might not be wasted, but instead will bring you glory. Amen.

PRAYER FOR THE CUP: Living God, loving God, forgiving God, we come by your invitation to drink of the love that you have freely poured out for us. We thank you for this lavish love, a love that we can't begin to comprehend. Help us live in a manner worthy of this love. Bless this cup that we raise before you, so that as we drink from it, we may truly feel the living Christ's presence in our lives. Amen.

UNIFIED PRAYER: In the silence of this special place, we come to receive precious gifts, gracious God. The bread we break and the cup we pour stand before us as symbols of our living relationship with Jesus Christ. Yet just as the disciples at the last supper worried about their own faithfulness and the faithfulness of one another, so we worry about ours. We know that we are not worthy and that we are here because of your grace. Yet through your Spirit, you make us worthy. Help us stand firm in that Spirit, so that we might not be afraid to witness to your love. Help us accept the grace that you have so freely given. Only then, we realize, will we know the full joy and peace of this table. Bless this bread and this cup, dear God, and through them may your Spirit transform us. Amen.

PRAYER AFTER COMMUNION: As we journey in faith as individual Christians and as a congregation, we thank you for this meal you have provided along the way. You have given us manna in the wilderness, and living water though our Lord Jesus Christ. Thank you, gracious God, thank you. Amen.

Proper 21
Sunday between September 25 and October 1

Exodus 17:1–7
Psalm 78:1–4, 12–16
Philippians 2:1–13
Matthew 21:23–32

PRAYER FOR THE BREAD: God of love and power, help us realize that we come to this table not only as individuals but as a community. Make us of the same mind. Lead us away from selfish, vindictive attitudes and help us look out for the interests of our brothers and sisters. As we share the bread here at your table, help us share a loving spirit as well. In breaking this bread, we look to Jesus Christ, who humbled himself to the point of death on a cross, so that we all might know your glory. Encourage us and guide us with your Spirit, so that we might witness to Christ's love. May our loving witness bring others to confess that Jesus Christ is Lord, to your glory. Amen.

PRAYER FOR THE CUP: We confess, mighty God, that we, like the Israelites in the wilderness, are a quarrelsome people. We confess also that there are times when we doubt your wisdom, presence, and power. And yet there is the miracle of water from the rock quenching the thirst of the people of Israel.

The cup on this table is a symbol of your wisdom, presence, and power. It is the miracle of the blood of your Son, Jesus Christ. This cup quenches our spiritual thirst.

By receiving the cup, we accept your forgiveness for the times we act in quarrelsome ways; we accept your forgiveness for doubting that you are always with us. Holy Spirit, we see the miracle of your power present in this gathering of Christ's people. Amen.

UNIFIED PRAYER: God of Moses, God of Jesus, God of each one of us, we come to you in prayer knowing that you hear us and that you care for us. We know that often we are untrusting and untrustworthy, but that you love us anyway. In coming to this table, we know that we have a lot to learn about love and unity, but we also know that you are our best teacher. Grant us humble spirits, so that we might have the same mind in us as is in Christ Jesus. Help us learn of Christ's self-giving nature as we break and eat this bread. Help us learn of Christ's love poured out for us as we bless and drink from this cup. Through your Spirit, help us exalt and glorify the name of Christ in all that we do. Amen.

STATEMENT AFTER COMMUNION: It is at this table that we have learned who we are and whose we are. We have learned love and acceptance at this table. We know that God is at work in us. The reign of God will take place as we go forth, looking to the interests of others, working for God.

Proper 22
Sunday between October 2 and 8
(World Communion Sunday)

Exodus 20:1–4, 7–9, 12–20 *Philippians 3:4b–14*
Psalm 19 *Matthew 21:33–46*

PRAYER FOR THE BREAD: O God who loves and guides us, you have given us laws and rules to live by. You spoke them to Moses on the mountain. They are so clear. Yet, God, we confess we have broken these laws many times.

We come to the table joining Christians all over the globe this World Communion Sunday in the knowledge that we have been forgiven. We join Christians of many colors, nationalities, and varieties of worship knowing that you have given us a Savior because you have loved us.

Many kinds of bread are on the tables around the world this day. But you are our only God; Christ is our Savior. These breads—broken as Christ's body was broken—are the symbol of your love and forgiveness and unity. Let us, as we eat of the bread, join in the celebration of this feast worldwide. Amen.

PRAYER FOR THE CUP: You ask us, God, to reexamine our lives and the things we have earned and possess. You ask us, God, to reexamine all that we are. And you ask us to know that all these do not compare at all to what you have given us in Christ Jesus.

We come to drink from this cup, knowing that gaining Christ Jesus our Lord surpasses anything we can ever earn or possess. Christ's resurrection makes this cup possible, and it is available for all.

Holy Spirit, keep us always striving for the heavenly goal. Amen.

UNIFIED PRAYER:

"What do you bring to Christ's table? We bring bread, made by many people's work, from an unjust world where some have plenty and most go hungry.

At this table all are fed, and no one is turned away. Thanks be to God.

What do you bring to Christ's table? We bring wine, made by many people's work, from an unjust world where some have leisure and most struggle to survive.

At this table all share the cup of pain and celebration, and no one is denied. Thanks be to God.

These gifts shall be for us the body and blood of Christ. Our witness against hunger, our cry against injustice, and our hope for a world where God is fully known and every child is fed. Thanks be to God."* Amen.

PRAYER AFTER COMMUNION: We thank you, God, for the gifts you give us: for the bread of our being loved, for the wine of our joy, for our life together as people ready to do the work of love and justice. And now we pray that, having been refreshed at this table, we may be bread and wine for each other and the world. Amen.**

*Eucharistic prayer by Brian Wren and Betsy King, "Let all the World," ed. Wendy Robins, quoted in *Bread of Tomorrow: Prayers for the Church Year,* ed. Janet Morley (Maryknoll: Orbis Press, 1992). Used by permission of Brian Wren.
**Barb M. Janes, "A Post-Communion Prayer," in *Pentecost, Summer, and Autumn,* vol. 3 of *Worship for All Seasons,* ed. Thomas Harding (Cleveland: The United Church Publishing House, 1994), p. 38. Reprinted with permission.

Proper 23
Sunday between October 9 and 15

Exodus 32:1–14
Psalm 106:1–6, 19–23
Philippians 4:1–9
Matthew 22:1–14

PRAYER FOR THE BREAD: O God of the Israelites and our God today, we confess that like those delivered out of Egypt, we sometimes forget you and worship other gods: time, money, good times. And yet, as Moses interceded for the Hebrew people, Jesus Christ has interceded for us. We know that in asking, we are forgiven. And we know that by eating this bread, the body of the very One who died for our sins, we realize this forgiveness.

As people renewed by forgiveness and nurtured by the bread of life, help us do justice and righteousness; help us always to worship you, the one God, in whom we receive life eternal. Amen.

PRAYER FOR THE CUP: "Finally, beloved, whatever is true, whatever is honorable, whatever is just, whatever is pure, whatever is pleasing, whatever is commendable, if there is any excellence and if there is anything worthy of praise, think about these things. Keep on doing the things that you have learned and received and heard and seen in me, and the God of peace will be with you."*

God, you have given us direction for the life of your body, the church. In Jesus Christ's name, we come to this table as a gathered community of believers. With our drinking from the cup comes the responsibility for

*Philippians 4:8–9.

the life of the church. Your son, Jesus Christ, gave his life so that we may live; let us live our lives in Christ's name. Amen.

UNIFIED PRAYER: O Giver of the most holy of banquets, we pray that we will always accept your invitation to this table willingly. Thank you for choosing us to be present today to celebrate this meal. We know that no one who comes to this table will hunger or thirst for you. You have generously given to us your Son, Jesus Christ, so that we will know you. Our hunger is satisfied, our thirst is quenched, our love knows no bounds, because of your love for us. Come, let us participate in God's banquet with thanksgiving. Amen.

STATEMENT AFTER COMMUNION: "Rejoice in the Lord always; again I will say, Rejoice…The peace of God, which surpasses all understanding, will guard your hearts and your minds in Christ Jesus."*

*Philippians 4:4, 7.

Proper 24
Sunday between October 16 and 22

Exodus 33:12–23
Psalm 99
1 Thessalonians 1:1–10
Matthew 22:15–22

PRAYER FOR THE BREAD: O God, you are great indeed! We give praise because you reign with justice, equity, and righteousness. We praise you most because you have given us a Savior in your Son. Through Jesus Christ, we experience forgiveness.

This bread, which we now eat together, is the visible symbol of the forgiveness of sins shown by the death and resurrection of Jesus Christ. In this meal, shared as the body of Christ, we experience not only your greatness and power but also your compassion and care.

Holy Spirit, lead us from this table to share the message that we have been given. Amen.

PRAYER FOR THE CUP: *(From 1 Thess. 1:1–10)*
God, we give you thanks for the countless generations of your followers who have spoken and lived the good news in Jesus Christ. By their dedication, courage, witness, and "steadfastness of hope in our Lord Jesus Christ," the gospel message lives today.

We can experience this good news in the presence of the Holy Spirit as we gather for this communion meal. The cup from which we will drink helps us remember the good news in a very tangible way. This is the cup of a living and true God who gave a son in death, and in so doing, gives us life. In drinking from the cup, we give you thanks and praise. Amen.

UNIFIED PRAYER: God of wisdom, we confess that there are so many things in our lives that we are tempted to put before you. It is sometimes hard to make choices about how we use our time, money, and talents. The world seems to demand so much of us.

Forgive us when we put those things of temporal value first. Give us wisdom to be discerning when decisions are required of us. Help us to find ways to serve you first.

At this table, we see the bread and cup and know that our Savior made a choice in our behalf. It wasn't the easy way or the worldly way, but the way of a God who loves all.

As we are strengthened physically and spiritually by this meal, give us the wisdom to choose your way in our lives. Help your faith live in us to be a witness to others making choices in their lives. Amen.

STATEMENT AFTER COMMUNION: We have just celebrated a time of grace, remembering God's presence in our spiritual journeys and how God was present in all parts of our being. We have been nourished by that undeservied love. It is time to go into the world and share that wonderful message with all God's people.

Proper 25
Sunday between October 23 and 29

Deuteronomy 34:1–12
Psalm 90:1–6, 13–17
1 Thessalonians 2:1–8
Matthew 22:34–46

PRAYER FOR THE BREAD: God of all ages and God ever new, be with us now. Your people gather at this table to celebrate the love of Christ that filled the upper room long ago, and the love of Christ that fills this room today. The bread that we break and eat now is a testament to the love that sustains us. Help us here so that we may learn by the example of our Lord Jesus Christ to love one another as we have been loved. Amen.

PRAYER FOR THE CUP: As we come to drink the cup of the new covenant, dear God, examine our hearts and spirits. Examine them not as a judge, but as a teacher and redeemer, so that we might grow more Christlike and loving. In receiving and acknowledging your grace, may we become more gracious. In receiving and acknowledging your compassion and forgiveness, may we become more compassionate and forgiving. Let this wine be a symbol of Christ's love for us, and of our transformation to the new life that you offer. Amen.

UNIFIED PRAYER: You are eternal, O God of the ages. Our years are few. You are all-powerful, O God of galaxies and quasars. We are weak and fragile. Yet, wonder of wonders, in your love and compassion, you care for us and give us a promise that we might live in you. Through the law and through the words of Jesus Christ, you have taught us to love you with all our hearts, and to love our neighbors as ourselves. At this table of communion, we recall that our Savior's actions spoke even louder than his words. In instituting this meal, in going to the cross, in rising from the dead, Christ demonstrated a love for you beyond our comprehension, and a love for us that conquered death itself. In eating this bread and drinking this wine, we affirm the power of Christ's love and seek to grow in our ability to love one another as you have loved us. Amen.

STATEMENT AFTER COMMUNION: A dying Moses looked across the river to see the promised land that he would never enter, yet it was enough. Here at this table, we have seen a glimpse of the reign of God, a preview of the resurrection promise that someday all God's children will inherit.

Proper 26
Sunday between October 30 and November 5

Joshua 3:7-17
Psalm 107:1-7, 33-37
1 Thessalonians 2:9-13
Matthew 23:1-12

PRAYER FOR THE BREAD: God, who calls each of us to obedience in faith, we come to your table as ones who are weak. Like Moses and Joshua, we too are called to obey you. Our faith is too weak to think you could use ones like us for your reign's purpose and fulfillment. Yet we know you see possibilities that we cannot. Let our faith, like the leaven in bread, rise and give us courage to obey your call.

In the eating of the bread, let us remember the obedience of your Son, Jesus Christ, and what it means for us. Let us go forth to lead a life worthy of you, who call us into your kingdom and glory. Amen.

PRAYER FOR THE CUP: How grateful we are, dear God, that your steadfast love endures forever. How grateful we are that your love has been poured out for us in Jesus Christ. How grateful we are that our redemption depends not on our own righteousness, but on your love. As we drink this wine, we recall this saving work of Christ and express thanksgiving for the covenant that we have received. Through your Spirit, help us follow you as faithful and loving children of the promise. Amen.

UNIFIED PRAYER: Let us give thanks to the Lord, for he is good! We know that this meal is but a foretaste of the meal we will share with our Savior in the fullness of time. This bread and cup is but an appetizer for the food in heaven, where there will be no end of the good things that our God has provided for us. We hunger for more, knowing our hunger and thirst will be satisfied because of the life, death, and resurrection of our Savior, Jesus Christ. Strengthened, we go from this table into the world to share the goodness of our Lord. Amen.

PRAYER AFTER COMMUNION: Lead us, O God, to serve in your name. Help us to spread your word. We listen for your call; give us faith to respond in obedience. Amen.

Proper 27
Sunday between November 6 and 12

Joshua 24:1–3a, 14–25
Psalm 78:1–7
1 Thessalonians 4:13–18
Matthew 25:1–13

PRAYER FOR THE BREAD: Merciful God, often we measure ourselves and others by what we own and by how much we have. Yet we know that you measure us by our hearts. Renew us and restore our hearts, dear God, that they might be sensitive to our neighbor's need and to injustice in the world around us. Help us realize that as you have shown compassion for us, so we should show compassion for others. We take this bread now, we break it, and we eat, in loyalty to our Lord Jesus Christ, who instituted this meal. Like little children in school, we learn here how to share. Teach us, through your Spirit, so that our holiness may be seen through our caring and compassion. Amen.

PRAYER FOR THE CUP: Your love has been poured out on all creation, dear God, through the work of Jesus Christ. You forgive. You care. You hear us when we pray, and our prayers help you renew the world. This cup we now lift reminds us of all the good gifts that you have poured out for us, but especially of your gift of Christ Jesus, whose love so perfectly matches yours. Let this cup of communion teach us to trust in love's sustaining power and to share your love with others. Teach us the secret of your grace, that in giving we receive and that in emptying ourselves in humble service we are filled with your love. Transform us through your Spirit, that we might be your faithful children. Amen.

UNIFIED PRAYER: We come to this table looking to the past, O God of Ages, remembering that Jesus Christ came among us, and reenacting the meal he shared with the disciples. We come to this table looking at the present, living God, knowing that through your Spirit, the living Christ is with us today, supporting us and sustaining us. As we eat and drink here, we pray that the bread and wine that we share will help us be more Christlike in our daily living. We come to this table looking to the future, steadfast God, knowing that someday we will eat bread and drink wine together in Christ's kingdom. Through the power of your Spirit, we ask that you will help us be your faithful, loving people, shaped by your presence in holy moments such as these. Amen.

STATEMENT AFTER COMMUNION: We are God's holy household, called into a covenant of love. We have honored that covenant with this meal of bread and wine. Now we go into the world, led by the Spirit, charged with honoring the covenant of love in our daily lives. May God bless us on our way.

Proper 28
Sunday between November 13 and 19

Judges 4:1–7
Psalm 123
1 Thessalonians 5:1–11
Matthew 25:14–30

PRAYER FOR THE BREAD: O Giver God, you have entrusted us with who we are and what we have. Too often, we ourselves take credit for our good lives and our earthly possessions. Forgive us when these attitudes seem to define us. Turn our hearts to realize that we are yours, and everything we have is a gift from you.

Our greatest gift is salvation and eternal life given to us by your Son's death and resurrection. We gather at this table knowing that it is you, not us, who has made this meal possible. In the breaking and eating of this bread, we celebrate new life made possible by our Savior, Jesus Christ. Help us to live our lives as a gift from you, having trusted us to live as children of the light. Amen.

PRAYER FOR THE CUP: O God, we ask your mercy for us in our times of distress, unease, and fear. We know that you are a merciful God; in faith we await your mercy.

Help us, then, to be merciful and forgiving to all your children; as we have been given, so let us give.

You have given us this cup, the very life of your Son. You have given us life on Earth in abundance and eternal life with you in heaven. As we drink of this cup, remind us of your mercy so that we may extend it to all those in our lives. Amen.

Unified Prayer: Like the early Christians, we still wait for your coming, O God. We wait and learn patience, hope, trust, presence, and action. We watch for your coming. Help us to be ready; help us to recognize you. We anticipate your coming as we come to communion this day. The bread and cup that are on this table tell us that you have indeed come and will come again. We recognize you in the body and blood of our Lord, Jesus Christ. We wait, with the Holy Spirit's presence, for the new coming and new reign on earth! In waiting, help us embrace the mystery and surprise of your great love. Amen.

Prayer after Communion: Fill us, God, with your love as we have shared in the bread and cup. Fill us, God, with the presence of the Holy Spirit as we gather here. Show us the day of the Lord, living in faith, hope, and love. Amen.

Proper 29
Sunday between November 20 and 26
(Reign of Christ Sunday)

> Ezekiel 34:11–16, 20–24   Ephesians 1:15–23
> Psalm 100   Matthew 25:31–46

PRAYER FOR THE BREAD: O Shepherd God, who seeks the best for all those in your care, we come to the table today to be fed. We seek physical nourishment satisfied by a steaming, yeasty loaf of fresh bread. We seek communal nourishment satisfied by your reign of justice. We seek spiritual nourishment satisfied by the body of our Savior, the bread of life itself.

Holy Spirit, come; be among us and fill us with power to help the reign of God come on earth. Amen.

PRAYER FOR THE CUP: "Make a joyful noise to the LORD, all the earth. Worship the LORD with gladness; come into his presence with singing. Know that the LORD is God. It is he that made us, and we are his; we are his people, and the sheep of his pasture."*

We are present to give thanks for Jesus Christ, his life given for us. We are present to drink from the cup of life, given for us. Thanks be to God, who is indeed good. Amen.

UNIFIED PRAYER: O God who has met the hopes and fears of all the years, we come to the table to celebrate the fulfilling of your earthly and eternal reign. The lessons from your holy word give us hope, encouragement, and challenges in carrying out your reign.

*Psalm 100.

We meet at this table those who are hungering for spiritual food as well as those who are hungering for a yeasty, warm loaf of bread. We meet at this table those imprisoned for crimes of violence as well as those who are imprisoned by circumstances. We meet at this table those who need a warm coat as well as those who need the warmth of human comfort and compassion. We meet at this table those who thirst for a cold drink of water as well as those who would drink thirstily from the cup of your love.

We confess that we have turned away from you as we have not served those in need. Forgive us.

We gather with all your people at this table. You have provided for our physical and spiritual nourishment in this bread and cup made holy by your Son, Jesus Christ. Holy Spirit, guide us with hope and encouragement to meet the challenges of your holy reign on earth. Amen.

PRAYER AFTER COMMUNION: The reign of God is here. We are fed, our thirst is quenched. We are ready to enter your gates.

> "Master, we shall sing your praises,
> Man of sorrows, God of power.
> For the measured march of seasons
> Shall at last bring in the hour
> When, as lightning leaps the heavens,
> You return to lead us home.
> You have promised, 'I am coming.'
> Swiftly, our Lord Jesus, come."* Amen.

*Hilary Jolly, "Millennium Hymn," quoted in *The Christian Century* 16 (September 22–29, 1999): p. 894.

Scripture Index

22:1–14	Proper 23
22:15–22	Proper 24
22:34–46	Proper 25
23:1–12	Proper 26
24:36–44	Advent 1
25:1–13	Proper 27
25:14–30	Proper 28
25:31–46	Proper 29
28:1–10	Easter Day
28:16–20	Trinity Sunday

Luke

1:47–55	Advent 3
2:1–14 (15–20)	Christmas Eve/Day
2:(1–7), 8–20	Christmas Eve/Day
24:13–35	Easter 3

John

1:1–14	Christmas Eve/Day
1:(1–9), 10–18	Christmas 2
1:29–42	Epiphany 2
3:1–17	Lent 2
4:5–42	Lent 3
7:37–39	Pentecost
9:1–41	Lent 4
10:1–10	Easter 4
11:1–45	Lent 5
13:1–17, 31b–35	Maundy Thursday
14:1–14	Easter 5
14:15–21	Easter 6
17:1–11	Easter 7
20:1–18	Easter Day
20:19–23	Pentecost
20:19–31	Easter 2

Acts

1:6–14	Easter 7
2:1–21	Pentecost
2:14a, 22–32	Easter 2
2:14a, 36–41	Easter 3
2:42–47	Easter 4
7:55–60	Easter 5
10:34–43	Epiphany 1, Easter Day
17:22–31	Easter 6

Philippians

1:21–30	Proper 20
2:1–13	Proper 21
3:4b–14	Proper 22
4:1–9	Proper 23

Colossians

3:1–4	Easter Day

1 Thessalonians

1:1–10	Proper 24
2:1–8	Proper 25
2:9–13	Proper 26
4:13–18	Proper 27
5:1–11	Proper 28

Titus

2:11–14	Christmas Eve/Day
3:4–7	Christmas Eve/Day

Hebrews

1:1–4, (5–12)	Christmas Eve/Day
2:10–18	Christmas 1

James

5:7–10	Advent 3

1 Peter

1:3–9	Easter 2
1:17–23	Easter 3
2:2–10	Easter 5
2:19–25	Easter 4
3:13–22	Easter 6
4:12–14; 5:6–11	Easter 7

2 Peter

1:16–21	Last Sunday after Epiphany